Frei Otto, Bodo Rasch: Finding form

Frei Otto, Bodo Rasch: Finding Form

Towards an Architecture of the Minimal

The Werkbund shows Frei Otto, Frei Otto shows Bodo Rasch

Exhibition in the Villa Stuck, Munich, on the occasion of the award of the 1992 Deutscher Werkbund Bayern Prize to Frei Otto und Bodo Rasch

Catalogue, scientific contributions and bibliography
edited by Sabine Schanz

Edition Axel Menges

Published by	Deutscher Werkbund Bayern,
	Frei Otto und Bodo Rasch
With special thanks to	Deutscher Werkbund Bayern
	Adelheid Gräfin Schönborn
	Antoinette Cherbuliez
	Gerd Pfafferodt
	Ingrid Otto
	Azeema Ally-Rasch
	Christine Otto-Kanstinger
	Institut für Leichte Flächentragwerke, Stuttgart
	The City of Munich
	Sonderkonstruktionen u. Leichtbau GmbH, Leinfelden
	Saudi Binladin Group, Jeddah, Saudi Arabien
	Hebel GmbH, Fürstenfeldbruck
	Koit, Rimsting
	Liebherr, Ehingen
	Maurer und Söhne, München
	Speedwave, Jettingen
	Stemmler, München
	Wilkhahn, Bad Münder
	World Centre, San Francisco

Edited by	Sabine Schanz
Authors	Frei Otto
	Bodo Rasch
	Gerd Pfafferodt
	Adelheid Gräfin Schönborn
	Sabine Schanz
Translation	Michael Robinson
Design and typsetting	Christian Mahn
	Sabine Schanz
	Rainer Holzapfel
	Ulrike Hattler
	Ute Fiedler
Photographic work	Gabriela Heim, IL
Repro and printing	AWS, WWS
Title picture	Pink-Floyd-Schirme, 1978
	Foto: Frei Otto
Font	"Atelier Warmbronn"

5. Edition 2006
© 1995 Edition Axel Menges
ISBN 3-930698-66-8

Contents

On the Presentation of the Prize,
Adelheid Gräfin Schönborn 8

Notes on the Werkbund Prize,
Notes on Frei Otto, Gerd Pfafferodt 9

Finding Form – on the Way to an Architecture
of the Minimal, Frei Otto, Bodo Rasch 13

Natural Constructions,
a Subject for the Future 15

Experiments 55

Tent Structures 73

Net Constructions 93

Pneumatic Constructions 113

Suspended Constructions 127

Arches, Vaults, Shells 135

Branched Constructions 157

Energy and Environmental Technology 167

Convertible Constructions 179

Umbrellas 187

Makkah and Madinah 199

Biographies 224

Notes 231

The Deutscher Werkbund Bayern awarded the Werkbund first prize to Frei Otto with the request that he nominate a meritorious individual to whom the prize would be passed on. Frei Otto chose Bodo Rasch.

The exhibition "Gestalt Finden (Finding Form), the Werkbund shows Frei Otto, Frei Otto shows Bodo Rasch" was linked with the prize.

The prize was awarded at the opening of the exhibition in the Villa Stuck in Munich on 21 May 1992.

The exhibition showed scientific fundamentals, working methods and numerous projects from the work of Frei Otto and Bodo Rasch.

Over 150 working models of the research and planning stages for built and unbuilt projects were arranged according to construction principles, as forms in architecture have always been classified according to structural characteristics.

Tent constructions, net constructions, convertible constructions and suspended roofs, pneumatic constructions, shells-reversible domes of the suspended forms, lattice shells and bifurcated constructions.

Models and experimental devices with small, simple apparatus show experiments for the introduction of physical self-forming processes. They represent ways of finding form for tents, rope constructions, sells, arches, domes, vaults, convertible roofs, bifurcations and space frames.

A lecture delivered by Frei Otto at the University of Stuttgart as part of federal research program "Natural constructions" gives an insight into his long years of basic research. It is an attempt to interpret nature by examining their constructions.

The exhibits come from the following archives: Atelier Frei Otto Warmbronn, Institut für Leichte Flächentragwerke der Universität Stuttgart, Architekturbüro Bodo Rasch, Leinfelden, Saudi Binladin Group, Jeddah, Saudi Arabia, Deutsches Architekturmuseum Frankfurt, SL-Sonderkonstruktionen und Leichtbau Gmbh, Leinfelden.

The exhibition was set up by:
Christof Blühdorn, Sabine Schanz, Atelier Frei Otto with Ingrid Otto and Dietmar Otto, Architekturbüro Bodo Rasch with Rainer Holzapfel, Jochen Schindler, Jakob Frick, Manfred Schmid, Andreas Stephan, Hans Nopper, Eberhard Felger, Jochen Plass.
The exhibition system was designed by Frei Otto for the 1981 "Natural Constructions" exhibition in Moscow.

The "Atelier Warmbronn" font

ABCDEFGHIJKLMNOPQRSTUVWXYZ
abcdefghijklmnopqrstuvwxyz / 0123456789

The "Atelier Warmbronn" font in this catalogue was designed by Frei Otto in 1950 and introduced as the studio script when he founded his Berlin studio in 1952. All drawings were done by hand with a stencil pen or indian ink fountain pen. The font was not fixed, and accommodated the broadest possible number of variations. For example, Frei Otto used it for a tomb inscription in lead type in 1956 and for a book cover in 1984.
Two sets of stencils were prepared for internal use in Atelier Warmbronn in 1978, one 3 mm high and one 6.5 mm high that have been used since then. 1985 saw a revision of the characters for a printable font for books and magazines, which is unpublished at the time of writing.
In 1987 Dietmar Otto revised the font for computer use. Further improvements and vectorization came in 1992 and designs were registered under the name "Warmbronn 1992".

I believe that imagination with its mysterious power is stronger than knowledge. Only human beings have dreams. I think they can be more important than facts. Human beings' hope is unique as well. I think that even experience is inferior to hope.

Frei Otto has shown us a way of the imagination, founded on knowledge. He has taken the liberty of dreaming, of breaking up the old thinking and proving facts. He has based his hopes on experience, and never given up. Here the Werkbund is trying to show one stage on his long and stumbling way. Werkbund members from all over the German-speaking area have analysed imaginings, dreams and hopes and captured the presented state of things in this package. We have chosen this kind of Werkbund prize for Frei Otto. The form could be quite different for the next prize-winner.

The Werkbund does itself honour by awarding the Werkbund prize to Frei Otto. And I think that Frei Otto is doing himself honour by passing it on to Bodo Rasch.

Notes on the Werkbund Prize
Notes on Frei Otto

Gerd Pfafferodt

I should like to use some general and some personal observations to show the thoughts behind this prize and thus the choice of Frei Otto and Bodo Rasch as winners.

Today the Bavarian Werkbund is awarding the Werkbund Prize for the first time. 50 Werkbund members were given an empty notebook and asked to fill it with notes on or for Frei Otto. These notebooks are his prize.

In Frei Otto the Werkbund is honouring a fellow human being who perceives his political responsibility and an architect who gives impetus across many disciplines for building that is suitable for human beings. Many colleagues proudly cite him as their mentor. If I draw on my Werkbund experiences it seems that nothing is more difficult for a person with highly developed ideas than to bow to a colleague's judgement. So as not just to appear to defer, as a first exercise in distancing themselves from their own thoughts. Frei Otto's Werkbund colleagues invest their trust in the prize-winner and ask him to pass the prize on to someone to whom he would like to draw attention. Frei Otto chooses Bodo Rasch.

The exhibition is intended to draw attention to processes that give Frei Otto's work a continuing and unique quality of its own. That is why the exhibition is called "Finding Form". Language indicates the activity: finding form. Can a person find something he cannot see? Can he look for something that he does not know? Words refer to experience. They are identical with it.

The "Notes on Frei Otto" are full of experiences that give us an idea of the person. The personally formulated impressions also show difficulties – and the unformulated ones indicate tensions that arise when public honours are awarded. Not everyone thinks at an award ceremony of the tissue of personal relationships, favours, calculation and chance from which the solid base for all this brilliance is formed. A title, even better the right prize, and there we have the gleam of an educated person who is equipped beyond the questions of his specialist subject with a profound sense of truth and political perspicacity. The public reacts with a warm haze of general benevolence. The Werkbund does not want to use Frei Otto to cover up its uncertainty. It expressly claims to be a forum for public discussion. It wants to make concepts familiar, to support them until their significance is perceived, and above all it wants a constant exchange of ideas with a large number of social groups. Its ambitions alone could not prevent the Werkbund from seeming amorphous from time to time. So many people are hoping today that this prize will become a thorn in the flesh, enough of a stimulus for the Werkbund to show its hand. Hackelsberger puts it like this: "The Werkbund is intervening. Its intervention serves the humanization of the every day for the sake of the liberty and dignity of the individual, for the sake of the preservation and improvement of general, but also of particular circumstances. The Werkbund does not open up careers; it offers a field of discussion for the sake of ideals of enlightenment that nothing has overtaken." And for that reason there is a disputation rather than an encomium and chamber music.

Thinking liberates. At first, anyway, then at some point it drives in the direction of its own activity. It takes strength to break through this. But what happiness when it happens! Let us call this happiness leisure. It is the prerequisite for being able to work in a way that embraces many disciplines. This is perhaps why we so seldom meet people who do not have to protect their authority in competing special disciplines by encapsulation but take delight in being curious with clear perceptions and a lively mind that is open to other people.

The architect builds his house. In this way name and work are linked. May he permit himself a detour? Does the goal he has set himself mean excluding other goals? Does a person who insists on his name have to see that his plans are realized?

Do you know the condition, a kind of ecstasy, of thinking something through further and further although it is never realized? The quality of the thinking changes. Criteria re-order themselves. Understanding becomes more important than production. Understanding also means perceiving why something cannot be realized. It becomes possible to anticipate the recognition of a form. This kind of thinking takes on a meditative character at some point, while hopping from idea to idea can appear extremely clever although it is exclusively cumulative.

"Strictly speaking all material objects are constructions of nature." – "Construction means something that has been put together, something built." "Death is inherent in everything that has been put together. Work unceasingly on your salvation."

The first statement is by Frei Otto. The second is an exhortation by Buddha. I don't want to force any connections out of these sentences. I place them alongside each other. They examine our inability to understand ourselves as an aggregate, as a transient accumulation of the most diverse particles. Yes, in the abstract that's clear enough. Do we experience it like that as well?

Let's console ourselves with something tried and tested. Whether it be the beautiful delusion that all nature's objects are optimal, or whether it be the insinuation that seems so real to us that nature is destructive, like us. Both points of view lead us and fortify us in inflicting conspicuous damage.

"What is that word, honour?" The swine among Shakespeare's characters, Sir John Falstaff, has no sense of honour. For this reason he has abolished the concept of honour for himself. For him concepts are words, and words are air. Shakespeare in his justice gives this chap so much spirit, wit and impudence that he becomes a loveable character. Or is it wisdom that such charm blossoms only from a lack of virtue? Men live and lived without this feeling of honour before and after Falstaff. And many people have had their breath taken away when they thought they recognized how systematically honour is being removed from the world. Because it seems that people without a sense of honour have to stamp on the concept of honour. They try to replace the loss with geniality. I once found this thought in Mauthner and have not forgotten it, for Falstaff's sake.

At the time when I had to work out the provisions of the prize and then became more familiar with Frei Otto's work and saw things about him in a different light – I began to feel a keener sense of the concept of honour. The filigree models in the exhibition cannot be taken in a rush, they cannot be reduced to a single striking line. I am experiencing a beautiful illusion. The constructions acquire their dignity when they are upright, just as human beings discovered their dignity when they finally stood up and took their eyes off the ground. But the feeling is real. This is how I imagine the well from which Frei Otto draws. His honesty enables a broad look at the multiplicity of nature. Respect develops. And that is his creative power.

From some point in my increasing familiarity it seemed compelling to me that his constructions are as they are. Bodo Rasch says that Frei is the only architect in Germany who does not have to try to find theoretical groundings for his constructions, but can justify them from his life. Not simply because nature's structural principles are taken up. It is said today that the roof in Montreal is a copy of a spider's web. But the roof was constructed before the constructors could see the analogy. They could not recognize the spider's web until they had built their roof. The form was determined beforehand. Can anyone perceive something before he knows it? At last I am no longer surprised when I find projects that can no longer be realized, unrealized and unusually realized constructions, strange experiments and surprising solutions, splendid celebrations, diverse activities and the search for simplification all described together. Mankind's dreams always feed on the memory of self-uplift. Frei Otto was an airman. He sometimes affected me like a bird. A director will be forgiven the assertion.

Frei Otto does not perceive himself as a teacher. But Bodo Rasch learned from him. He works with his theory, realizes in other cultures, looks for new links and experiences a spiritual component that Frei Otto does not formulate.

If it is a basic right to be recognized for one's work then a prize can be a sign that it has been realized precisely here. Two people who were obviously looking for each other have found each other.

In fairy-tales prizes look like this: a heroic deed wins a princess, and decent work still gets a "cudgel in the sack". The bliss that also lies in the fairy-tale prize is clearly an extension of powers. The actual challenge is living with the prize. There is an increasing necessity to show oneself clearly. Prize-winners become kings. And so in the context of a prize award we experience an overlarge, overwrought gesture, we sense how profoundly the basic right to recognition can have been injured. Because it could also be that someone who shows himself clearly today cannot be used at will tomorrow. And the day after tomorrow he will not fit into the picture at all. A career needs elasticity and a quality of conforming. And thus careers produce faces that are only tired, otherwise life has left no traces behind. Lack of life seeks publicity, eternity instead of life. And we long for blues singers and story-tellers whose living faces are earnest of the experiences they can pass on so wonderfully.

Can we still clear up how we are mutually making idiots of ourselves, who thinks who is stupid or is being passed off as stupid, or who is making everything stupid for whom? Experts, politicians, parties, boards etc. There is a hint of that in the notes about Frei Otto as well.

Primitive architecture was an architecture of necessity. It used nothing to excess, no matter whether it was stone, clay, reeds or wood, animal skins or hair. It is minimal. Even in poverty it can be very beautiful and is good in the ethical sense. Minimal primitive architecture can be structure and ornament at the same time. Decoration makes sense if it is essential.

Good architecture is more important than beautiful architecture. Beautiful architecture is not necessarily good. The ideal is ethically good architecture that is also aesthetic. Buildings that achieve this ideal are rare. Only they are worth keeping.

We put up too many buildings. We squander space, land, mass and energy.
We destroy nature and cultures. Buildings are an exercise of power, even if we do not intend it, because we cannot do otherwise. The contrast between architecture and nature is getting bigger and bigger,
We have too many buildings that have become useless and yet we still need new buildings, from pole to pole, in the cold and in the heat, we need them to be mobile and immobile.
Man's present areas of settlement are the new ecological system in which technology is indispensable, even in hot and cold areas. Thousands of kinds of plants and animals coexist with human beings in a new way in this system. The dominant species is homo sapiens.
Nevertheless we still build the unnatural buildings of past epochs. Our times demand lighter, more energy-saving, more mobile and more adaptable, in short more natural buildings, without disregarding the demand for safety and security.
This logically leads to the further development of light constructions, to the building of tents, shells, awnings and air-supported membranes. It also leads to a new mobility and changeability. A new understanding of nature is forming under one aspect of high performance form (also called classical form), which unites aesthetic and ethical viewpoints. In this context we recognize the quality of native buildings and settlements.
To solve today's problems we need the new integrated architecture of the ecological system of the earth's surface that is settled by man. Using the insights of all sciences the finding-form of this

new, peaceful, self-settling system will be encouraged first of all by the fact that resistances are broken down. Reducing the buildings and roads that are forming a crust over the surface of the earth is part of this.

Many people hope that the new architecture of the minimal will encourage peaceful cohabitation and make social self-regulation processes possible. The prerequisites for this are in place, because dwellings, buildings and settlements will again be designed by the hands of the people who live in them, to the benefit of nature and mankind. But present-day architecture is still an instrument of the exercise of power.

Tomorrow's architecture will again be minimal architecture, an architecture of the self-forming and self-optimization processes suggested by human beings. This must be seen as part of the new developing ecological system of the people who have densely and peacefully settled the surface of the earth. It is an architecture that respects genuine traditions and the multiplicity of forms in animate and inanimate nature. The exhibition is intended to make suggestions aimed at this distant goal and draw attention to its consequences. Development is shown, not the finality of the perfect. The working material shown makes no claims to completeness and shows the bases and methods of finding form within the framework of our way of working. The way shown, which can perhaps at some time lead to an architecture of the minimal, is simply one among many.

Natural Constructions, a Subject for the Future

Construction means bringing things together, building them. All material objects are constructions. They consist of parts and elements. This is true of the whole cosmos, at natural objects and of those made by man. Processes bring about this act of putting things together into a construction. Processes bring about change. Countless objects exist. Countless objects come into being and pass away again.

Natural constructions are not just any objects of infinitely variable diversity for us. We are looking for those constructions that show with particular clarity the natural processes that create objects. We are looking for the essential. We even speak of the "classical" when something that cannot be improved becomes visible.

Although technology is a tool of man, who asserts himself against all the rest of nature by using technology against nature, we nevertheless understand it as a product of the natural object man and thus also as a part of nature. He has simply made use of it for himself. Now at last he recognizes that he is disturbing, damaging, destroying her. He is increasingly looking for ways of preserving her. He tries to be a part of nature, a part of the whole. His means is technology that is compatible with nature.

Our research group is trying to use the observation of the processes by which constructions come into being to recognize the whole, in other words the coexistence and being within each other of many objects.

Research:

Architects, civil engineers and biologists worked together on this research topic from the beginning. Then came philosophers and historians and finally physicists and synergeticists. This makes the federal research program 230 one of the most interdisciplinary research groups in the world. The processes of self-formation of objects are the object of our most recent research.

The times are past in which people believed that the world was increasingly sinking into chaos, into an anarchy of nature. We

Text of a lecture by Frei Otto to a symposium of the SFB 230 federal research program on 1. 10. 1991 at the University of Stuttgart.

The "Biology and Building" research group was founded in Berlin in 1961 and found a permanent home at the University of Stuttgart in 1964. It worked intensively on membrane and net constructions, from 1970 as part of the federal research program 64 of the Deutsche Forschungsgemeinschaft, and then from 1985 in the federal research program 230 which deals with natural constructions.

ask: is there such a thing as lasting, enduring, comprehensive chaos? Is chaos not a passing condition of nature, in order for processes of order to begin at all?

Intermediate chaotic states are natural. Partial catastrophes create partial chaos. This makes renewal possible. If many material objects form of their own accord, in other words without being made by man, then they count as natural.

All material, natural objects are formed by processes, and these can be recognized from the form of the objects. Many processes and their products are independent of the material, incidentally. Often the same processes take effect despite different materials, and then produce similar objects. For example, whatever material heavenly bodies are made of, they always become spherical with increasing size.

Artificial – natural:

Man-made objects are artificial according to our use of language, but this is not always true for art. Artificial objects can also have natural components. This is especially true when self-forming physical processes occur of their own accord or are deliberately activated in the manufacture and planning of technical objects.

Technical objects for which self-formation processes occur to a high degree form the natural border between natural and artificial.

Art objects are man-made and thus artificial. And yet they can also, like all purely technical objects, have come into being as a result of natural processes.

We live at a time in which the span of the artificial and also of art is growing at a tempestuous pace. On the one hand art is becoming more artificial than it ever was, but on the other hand more natural as well. Then art can become nature.

Made-up nature:

Today there is such a thing as made-up nature. Man can strive to shape nature in the image of a nature he has made up himself. It is easier to speak and write about made-up nature than about true nature.

We look for the real, natural objects that we have to see and touch if we want to grasp them. What we perceive are symbolic images. Then again the images are an aid to further observation. They are images from our life, from our cosmos, as we can see, measure and touch it. Only images we have grasped ourselves are close to the truth. Words are blunt and imprecise.

We try to grasp objects of the macrocosm and the microcosm afresh as well. They are objects that in most cases cannot be explained by the knowledge of physics, chemistry and biology alone. They are actually the quite everyday objects that were once the main object of the early sciences, but which have ceased to be topical because of the strong inclination to mathematics and the so-called exact sciences.

The current task:
Concern for the self-formation processes that make everyday things is in the news again. Nature is increasingly observed processually and integrally. Our distant aim is better understanding of the larger systems. A beginning is made with the most important components of the ecological systems.
Our subject is delicate because it fits almost too well into this time of a new openness to ecology which unfortunately often becomes a fashion, because everything that has the syllables "bio" or "eco" in its name is considered good. Almost nobody has any doubts about this and yet it is not true. Ecology and biology are not good, and they are not evil either. Nature is neither good nor evil. Only we and our products can be good or evil.

The architects' task:
Normally the aim of the architect is to produce architecture. They have forgotten how to research. And yet latterly architects have committed themselves to research as never before. Instead of planning buildings or cities they now want to pursue the processes of change and self-origin in man-made objects quite generally.
The biotope building, the city as an ecological system, the way to the minimal mass building, to the minimal energy building, that is at one with the landscape and at the same time architecture, is to be found. The task is a difficult one. Solutions are hardly to be expected, as there is no such thing as the building and the city. There is just an infinite number of houses and cities that can all be approximately optimal in terms of energy in a way that is suitable for their time. Even in the field of classical form, which is at the end of a development series, and to which nothing more can be added or taken away, there is rarely only the one conclusion. The search for the natural in architecture does not restrict the possibilities, it extends them. It creates the condition that our buildings can for once be less unnatural than they have been previously.
The artists in our research, the valiant representatives of architecture, are on the way to making their art less unnatural and thus closer to nature and perhaps are stepping along the first path to a new kind of architecture that is based on research into

nature among other things. Architects want to find out scientifically where there is a new link between nature and building.

In some fields technical products have been found in this way that also count as explanatory models for living constructions. This was the case with tyres, bifurcations and nets. It is worth doing some more work here.

Architects are pursuing the classical route of inventing, designing and developing technical objects. This way is clearly prescribed and comprehensible in every phase. It can be used to establish whether the resulting products are more energy-saving, lighter, more flexible and closer to human beings.

This way can sometimes lead to products that are both high-performance technical products and, as they frequently contain an aesthetic component, also represent a link with the art of building.

Architects feel, not as ideologues but on the basis of their research, that it is sensible for the preservation of the living space of our species to keep the large ecological systems like forest, water, city free of all ballast and especially from the excess of our buildings, transport systems and machines. They hope that their urban architecture will give the new ecological system of the human beings' city a basis for long-term survival.

The biologists' task:
Since Gerhard Helmcke's initiatives at the Technical University in Berlin around 1960 biologists have been working on the subject of simultaneous consideration of the natural quality of human constructions and those of living nature. The focal point of their commitment was the physical and mechanical processes that lead to the emergence of life and which, alongside genetic reproduction, still shape the form of living objects, which are not explicable without this self-forming, fundamentally abiotic process. Even in the preparatory stages of this research thoughts were taken up again that had already appeared in the previous century and been rejected . In about 1970 they led to a completely new way of observing nature on the basis of new perceptions about membrane and net construction supported by internal pressure. A significantly refined picture of the shaping of animate matter began to emerge as a result: all living creatures are built with a single construction and appropriately belong to a single formal canon.

Explanations are still being sought in the same way today with the indubitably extremely important thought model of genetics. Additionally it is extremely difficult to integrate insights into synergetics that have since been found about self-ordering processes and the experiences of engineers and architects when designing mass- and energy-optimized construction into the new picture of the emergence of form.

The complex observation of living objects in their behaviour to each other and as the partners of large systems is becoming even more difficult. Particular attention is needed here for research into the ecosystem of the human city, a system that can be considered only by the co-operation of biologists, urban developers, behaviour researchers and engineers. This also needs the inclusion of the simultaneous running of different processes that influence each other and which despite much conflict and despite constantly occurring partial catastrophes can still create a long-lasting, stable system.

Task of the engineering scientists:
Their task is to research the mechanics of self-formation in the sphere of this subject, because there are forces operative in the self-forming constructions that can bring about synthesis, change and destruction.

The engineering constructions of towers, bridges and houses, of roads, railways and canals change both at the design stage and under construction. They also age after that and finally become ruins if they are not adapted or renovated.

The process of seeking form for large engineering constructions can serve as a model for the future explanation of forces and force transpositions in objects of an animate and inanimate nature. It is a first stage in the explanation of the origin of their form.

Processes occur in the development of extreme engineering constructions in which spontaneous ideas can be optimized gradually. These processes have a life of their own. They are dependent of the people who set them in motion, but often produce results that were not predictable, indeed are even surprising.

Some of these optimization processes in engineering science are entirely similar, and in part identical with some self-formation processes in inanimate nature and the selection processes of animate nature, which are natural as far as our determination of concepts is concerned.

Engineering constructions are a particular burden on their environment even if they are considered good in technical and human-ethnological terms. They often destroy grown biotopes and inflict severe damage on ecosystems. They are not just said to be extremes of unnatural building, they actually are. However, we still need them. We hope that many of them will be superfluous in future. Engineers' tasks are changing today. It is increasingly their task to reduce buildings even at the planning stage and to remove superfluous buildings carefully by using their thinking, ideas, inventions and research. It is their task to fit every unavoidable new structure into its environment with a minimum of materials and energy consumption in such a way that it becomes part of an ecological system.

Task of the exact scientists:
The pioneers of synergetics helped us to perceive that there is a balance in inanimate nature between objects that decay, implode or explode, dissolve or are destroyed and those that re-form themselves.
Inanimate nature is not disintegrating, as was once postulated, to the point of chaotic unecognizability. It is in a state of permanent transformation. Something that is briefly chaotic constantly rearranges itself into new objects and constructions. It forms the new shapes of natural constructions.
With their – in fact still very imperfect – knowledge about the self-formation of objects synergeticists are already attempting synthetic tasks. They research each event in which several or indeed many self-formation processes are effective simultaneously, inanimate, biological and technical. Here a way of grasping large systems is being sought.
The number of resulting possibilities is visibly so unimaginably large that new thought models are needed to grasp the many processes and combinations of processes that form complex and new objects.
The most important object of synergetic research is our own ecosystem, the settled surface of the earth, the city. But this system cannot be grasped without knowledge of the self-formation and self-ordering processes of its elements.

Task of the scholars in the humanities:
Analysis of the concept of "nature" is a key task for philosophers. It is about time we finally found out what nature is today and by that I mean the real nature in which we live which we reshape, shape and alienate whether we like it or not.
In the mean time it has become clear that what Aristotle, Plato, Kant, Hegel and Schelling said about nature may be very clever and may have been appropriate to the times in which these great philosophers lived, but it does not describe real nature, it tries to find words for a nature that they have devised for themselves.
What use is devised nature to an architect when housing hoards of

homeless people? What use is devised nature to an engineer faced with avoidable natural catastrophes? Both of them are dealing with r e a l nature.

Part of current philosophy is a humanities subject for nature models that are no longer topical. Physicists, doctors, architects, engineers are working on new nature images. This makes them the real philosophers of today. They do not arrive at o n e understanding of nature, but many. Ultimately every consciously living human being has his own!

Current real philosophy is in the act of turning its gaze forwards. It has begun to search for our current image of nature. Despite all the differences and diversity, outlines are beginning to emerge.

We already need prognoses for the 21st century image of nature. We must all work on it: humanities scholars and natural scientists, biologists, engineers, architects and everyone who is concerned with nature and man.

This also goes for artists and especially for professional politicians as well. They are the motor for pragmatic changes within our multiform voting society.

Like philosophy, the humanities too must come up to date. Look at everything that has happened since 1950 and at what unique insights into the nature of thing and man-made constructions are arrived at every day!

What all researchers and artists have achieved on the complex theme of nature and the ways that they have taken to do this must be documented, ordered and thought about by our own witnesses today and not at third hand.

The present day is moving enormously and in a way that can scarcely be grasped, as it never has before. This movement is itself a great process of self-ordering and creation of form. Without historians' work on the events of the day we shall not succeed in perceiving the processual quality of our times in its totality. Later historians will be faced with insoluble problems without the preliminary and basic work that must be done now.

Conclusion:

"Self-formation" and "Natural Constructions" are subjects that need a great deal of commitment. Research into them needs strong collective leadership. It is endangered if the researchers involved think exclusively of their own narrow subject area, if they forget that they must always see things as a whole. Work on the subject of "Natural Constructions" goes on. What has been done so far is only a tiny part of what has to be done. The most important, as yet still provisional, result is a new interpretation of life's origin and the acquisition of form. Future work requires insights into the formation of objects, of emergence from an unordered state, of creation. It must occur through objective, level-headed research with a clear aim.

And yet, all work that goes beyond the boundaries of a discipline and therefore is undisciplined from the point of view of the disciplines, will always have a subjective component. It is done by people who make great mental efforts, who often tear down the boundaries of disciplines but unintentionally build new walls. It is done by people who constantly need motivation.

A new, subjective, quite personal understanding of nature can be a motivation. I observe with greatest respect what is happening before my eyes, especially the things that are fundamentally independent of man's unnatural acts. I also thus acquire a new relationship to those man-made, artificial things that make it possible to see some reduction in the unnatural. For me a new understanding of nature, technology and art is starting to appear on the horizon.

But we human beings still do not see nature. We still think of nature and find devised nature as a reflection of ourselves. We shape nature according to wishes that derive from devised nature. In this way we alienate nature, make it artificial and still do not get art. We often torment what is living without noticing. We are destroying our world, which we do not recognize because we are blind.

Frei Otto

The Birth of Form
A Picture History

Material objects acquire their form through processes that shape form. Forms originate in all natural spheres:
– in inanimate nature
– in animate nature
– in animal and human technologies
– in art

All material objects in nature and technology have form and are put together; thus they are constructions.
Natural objects are natural constructions. They come into being as a result of self-formation processes.
Man can both stimulate natural processes and also do artificial things.

Self-formation Processes in Inanimate Nature

Since the birth of the universe, the stars and the planets have formed and passed away; they range in size from the infinitesimal to immense.

1 Heavenly bodies
Liquid balls as a result of gravity.

2 Stars and galaxies in the universe
Rotating heavenly bodies.

3 Large-scale weather systems
Vortices caused by spinning masses of air.

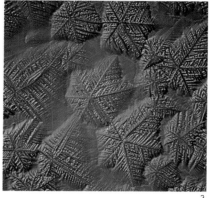

1 Crystallization
Self-ordering as a result of molecular forces.

2 Contraction strain cracks caused by cooling (basalt).

3 Surface decoration
Crystal formation on surfaces (lead sulphide).

4 Shrinkage cracks
caused by drying (clay).

1

2

3

4

5

6

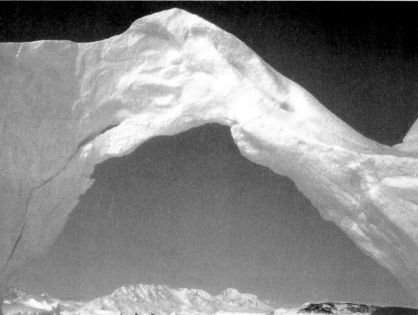

1 Pebbles
rounded by running water (beach).

2 Travelling dunes
ribbed by the wind.

3 Wind erosion
by temperature variations and sandstorms.

4 Earth towers
caused by rain erosion.

5 Erosion
rain and water shape rock.

6 Rock arch
caused by thermal stress and water erosion.

7 Rock tower
caused by thermal stress, horizontal
stratification and water erosion.

8 Mountains
dough-like layers, folded by lateral pressure.

9 Ice arch
caused by thawing.

10 Cone shapes
caused by friction and gravity when scree
was released by water and temperature
fluctuations.

1

2

3

4

5

1 Natural pneumatic
drop formed by surface tension.

2 Creeks and rivers
water transport in concentrated path
systems.

3 Suspended drop of mercury
formed by surface tension and gravity.

4 Lightning
concentrated path systems for electrical
energy.

5 Clouds
made up of countless water droplets.

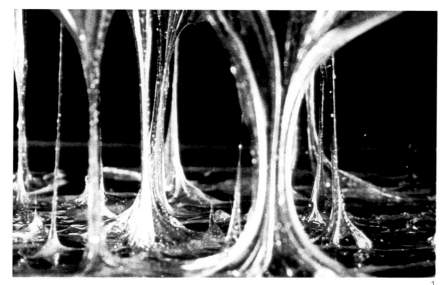

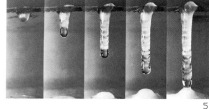

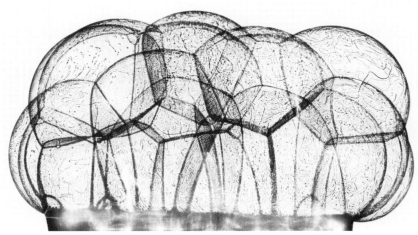

1 Viscous masses
formation of bubbles and columns (e.g. when
the temperature of rock is raised).

2 Congealed drop of liquid
(moon rock).

3 Free-floating bubbles
caused by internal pressure and membrane
tension.

4 Bubble cluster and foam
linked pneumatics.

5 Icicles
freezing water droplets.

6 Stalactites and stalagmites
caused by water drops and minerals.

Animate Nature

Animate nature "uses" a lot of inanimate nature's self-formation processes like the formation of small bubbles, threads and patterns, but it differs fundamentally from inanimate nature in that her objects die and ultimately become dead natural objects.

Animate objects reproduce by division and sexual multi-plication. They changed as a result of random mistakes in reproduction and "develop" through the untargeted "optimization process" of negative selection through an inability to survive. More and more diverse forms emerge with ever more marked abilities to dominate other living crea-tures.

1

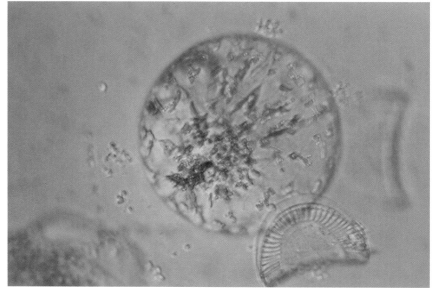

2

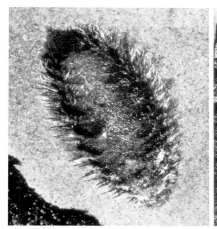

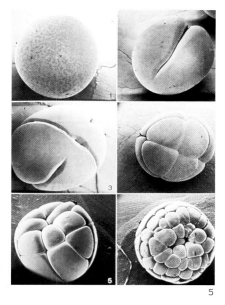

3

5

4

1 Microsphere
as yet inanimate cell, constructive element
of life.

2 Living cells
in terms of construction are fibre-supported
balloons filled with liquid.

3 Multicellular primeval creatures.

4 Taut spherical pneumatics (berries).

5 Reproductive multiplication
cell division.

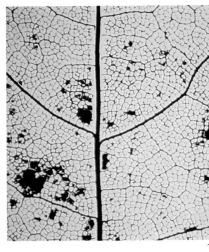

1 Path systems for juices and forces (e.g. leaves).

2 Increased hardness from silicia fibres (grasses).

3 Ramification in non-woody plants.

4 Trees
hardening by high fibre-density and conglutination (wood).

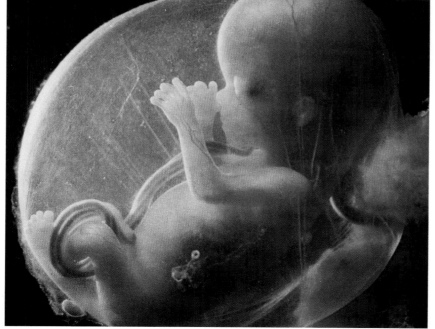

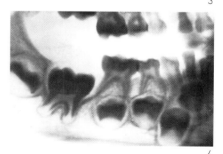

1 Ramification constructions in animal colonies: corals.

2 Pneumatics in the pneumatic, the bone skeleton starts to harden (human foetus).

3 Soft body partially hardened by hard substance inclusion.

4 Spherical pneumatics in the jaw tooth formation.

Animal and Human Technologies

For about half a million years highly developed and mobile animals have been using technologies for shaping products.

Techniques used by insects and spiders, whose forms and constructions are anchored genetically, are old in terms of biological development.

Genetic anchoring is increasingly replaced by learning from parents in higher animals and those that are younger in terms of biological development. Tools and materials that are part of the body are supplemented by found items or tools the animal makes itself.

Finally man invents and develops technical objects according to his own targeted optimization processes with self-reproducing tools that create products from self-made materials in any quantity and only exceptionally relate to animate natural objects or animal technologies.

Technical objects age and become superfluous. They are replaced by technically improved items. Art objects are produced using technologies.

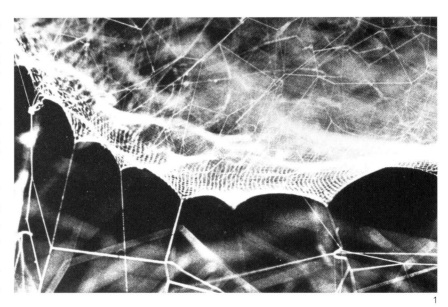

1

2

They are frequently a very great distance away from all nature. They do not need models, rules or conventions. They develop very little or not at all.

3

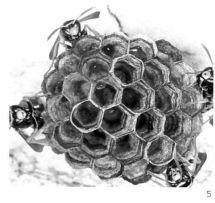

5

4

1 Animal technologies
spiders' webs, devices for catching food, overall genetically anchored.

2 Spiders' webs in detail
hardened forms of viscous thready masses.

3 Birds' nests
houses for vertebrates, built from found material.

4 From inside a termite city
three-dimensional light construction.

5 Wasps' nest
miniature city built of self-made paper.

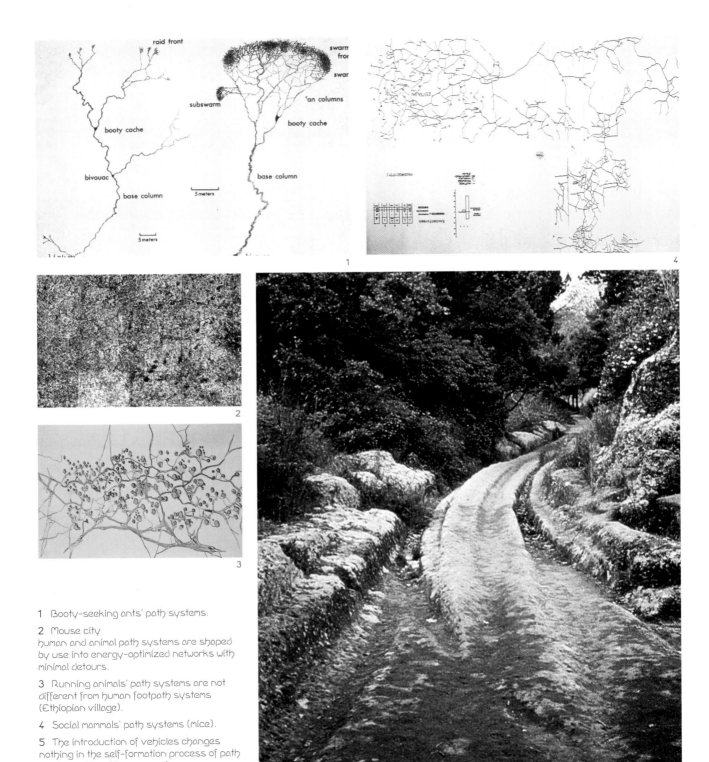

1 Booty-seeking ants' path systems.

2 Mouse city
human and animal path systems are shaped
by use into energy-optimized networks with
minimal detours.

3 Running animals' path systems are not
different from human footpath systems
(Ethiopian village).

4 Social mammals' path systems (mice).

5 The introduction of vehicles changes
nothing in the self-formation process of path
systems either (Roman road).

1 Occupation of area and path system in a medieval town centre.

2 Area occupation when distance is to be kept is identical in humans and animals.

3 Occupying the surface: excessively dense settlement.

4 The primeval house protection from the weather: reed hut.

5 More highly developed building technology woven reed hut.

1 Primeval house in stone
dry-stone dome.

2 The great dome of antiquity
planned building form in applied geometry
(Pantheon, Rome).

3 Clay dome
classical form of vaulting.

4 Early ashlar dome in a conical shape.

5 Tower foundation in the fortress at
Jericho, about 8000 years old.

6 Tower of Babel, vision of 1567.

1 The arch
used for at least 4000 years
(Cordoba, Spain).

2 Suspension bridge
known from the earliest times, self-formation
by the rope.

3 Fishing nets
like tents acquire their shape by self-
formation.

4 Iron bridge
200 years old, minimum use of materials.

5 Suspension bridge
a type that is still built today.

1

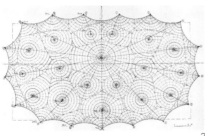

2

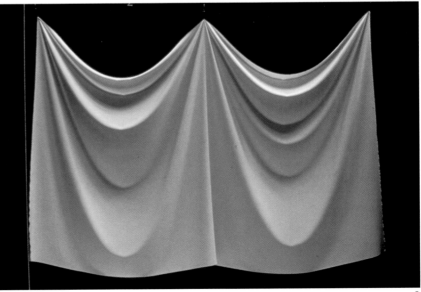

3

1 Folding membrane roof.

2 Regularities in the fold diagram of a roof

3 Folds in suspended sheet.

4 Pneumatic
floating hose as a pedestrian bridge.

5 Fold formation in crumbled foil.

6 Pneumatic: hot-air balloon.

6

Self-formation Processes Used by Man

5

When objects form of their own accord man can make direct use of the process. For example, when building up ramparts and embankments he will take account of the angles of natural embankments. he can work out the shape of arches from spiders' webs or the shape of bowls from suspended nets. There is a new form of self-formation process, using computer optimization pro-grammes to find solutions for practical problems.

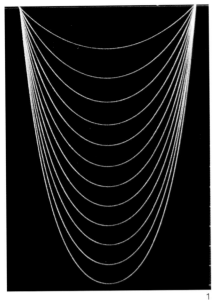

1

2

3

4

5

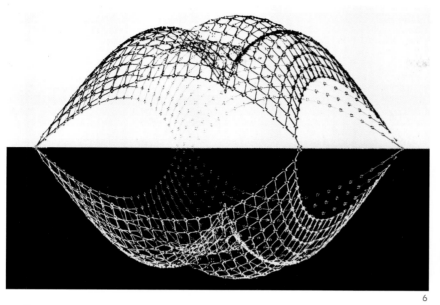

6

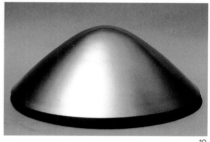

10

7

1 Suspended chains
a model for standing arches.

2 "Standing" chain line
(the Super-Arch in St. Louis, USA).

3 Self-adjusting arch of a chain with links.

4 Use of self-formation in earthworks
(spoil tipping).

5 Self-formation in well-building
(experimental self-formation of a cistern
hollow).

6 Suspended nets as a model for grid shells.

7 Soap film between threads
model for the four-point tent.

8 Soap film with high point
model for a high-point tent
(e.g. the Institute for Lightweight Structures
at the University of Stuttgart).

9 Threads and soap film
model for a pointed tent.

10 Ideal form of the dome
self-formation using computer calculation
after a model experiment.

8

9

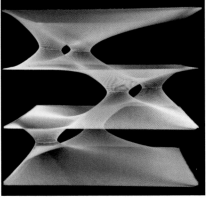

1 Soap film, model for a tent.

2 Self-formation of a soap film in the wir, sail shape.

3 Self-formation of a sail
by air pressure and cut, optimization by soap film experiment and computer calculation.

4 Nets in a three-dimensional arrangement as an explanation of spatial networks.

The Reverse Path

The "reverse path" method makes it possible to recognize formation processes in animate and inanimate nature to the extent that such processes are set in motion artificially. This is done by experiment and the technical development of constructions. Technical developments driven forward at a high level of qualification permit better knowledge of nature's non-technical constructions. This is known as the reverse path. Nature is not copied, but made comprehensible through technical developments.

For example, technical and scientific development work on electricity and water supplies and on load-transmitting skeleton constructions produce broadened knowledge about the flow of water in streams and rivers and the flow of electrons in lightning flashes. And it also brings early insights into the origin and genetic fixing of leaves, shrubs, trees and corals.

One important result of work with the reverse path is that systematic research and technical development of pneumatic constructions made of tissue-supported membranes for use in halls with very wide spans produced significant progress in explaining the origin of life and the shaping processes. The preceding analytic basic research in the last 200 years was not able to do this as it did not know the formation processes of technical pneumatic constructions.

It was clearly recognizable that animate nature applies the abiotic self-formation process of bubble formation, and additionally that complex fibre networks of the kind used by technology are necessary and are then found in nature. It is clear: the fibre-supported soft pneumatic structure is life's primitive construction. It forms cells, organs and living creatures as a whole, even when parts harden and for example form wood or bone.

The process of biological reproduction that divides the animate from the inanimate uses an abiotic building element. It could not function without this. The abiotic element needed when living organisms acquire shape is considerable, larger than anticipated. however, it decreases with increasing perfection in terms of evolutionary history.

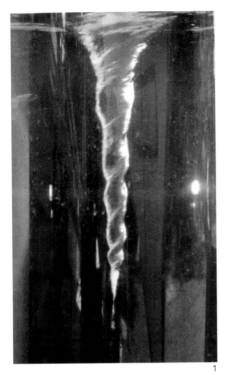

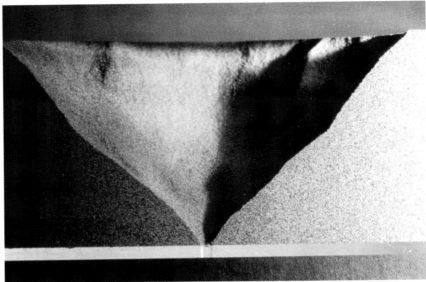

1 The formation of vortices in liquids helps to explain tornadoes.

2 The study of funnel formation helps to understand crater formation.

3 Cones and craters made up of scree.

4 Bubbles covering a surface.

5 Surfaces covered by bubbles explain crystal constructions and also the formation of biological patterns.

6 Specks of fat of various sizes demonstrate surface occupation.

7 Direct path system
minimal energy consumption, large path lengths. Large land use (thread net model).

8 Minimal path system
shortest possible overall path length, linked with detours. Small surface use (self-formation with soap films).

9 Energy optimization by limited detours (self-formation in damp thread network).

10 Shrinkage cracks in concrete extension of knowledge about cracks and defects in earth and rock.

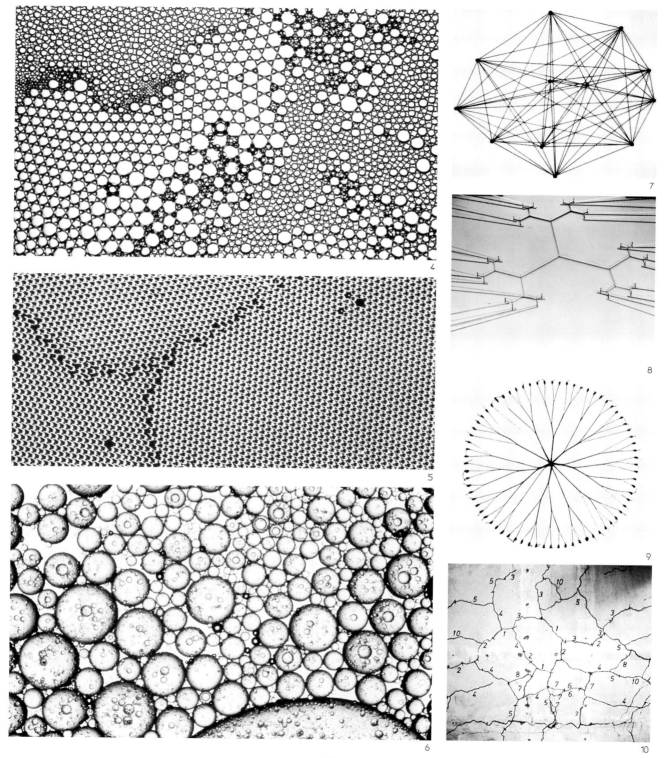

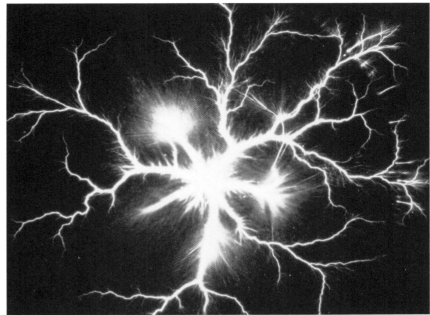

1 Cells are liquid-filled containers, in technical language: fibre-supported "pneus" - pneumatic constructions.

2 The classic "pneu", the free-floating soap bubble, identical in form with the microsphere and the primitive cell.

3 Energy optimization by concentration (artificial electrical discharge).

4 Three-dimensional branching structure as support for a wooden tent (Bad Dürrheim).

5 Computer-generated path systems and branching constructions.

6 Net forms in pneumatic constructions experiment.

7 Fibre network of a cell (cytoskeleton).

8 Strain folds in thick skins not genetically fixed.

9 Tangled fibres drawn apart in an experiment, produce the structural forms typical for nets in cells.

10 Bubble and net formation in a living cell (radiolaria).

11 Bubbles on a sphere.

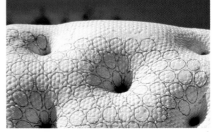

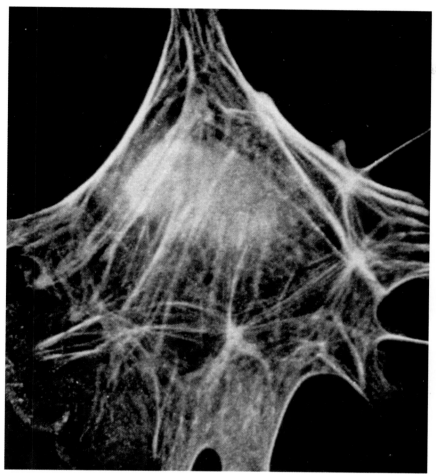

7

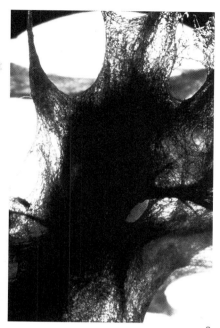

9

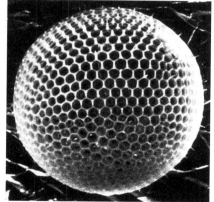

10

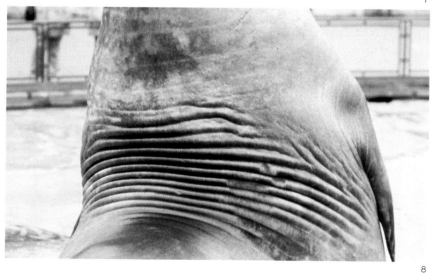

8

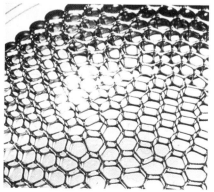

11

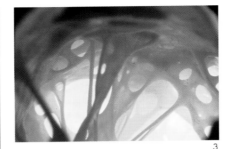

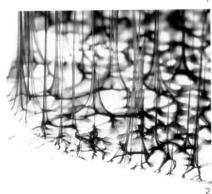

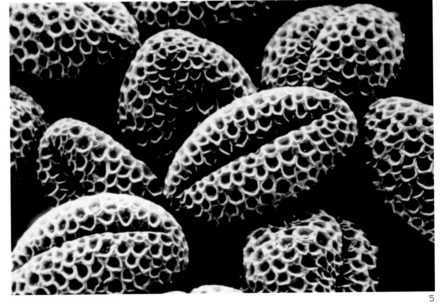

1 Experiments with damp three-dimensional fibre nets lead to exploration of bone constructions etc.

2 Drawn-out tips of plastic masses are found in the same form in living creatures (e.g. radiolaria).

3 Forms of thread-drawing or membrane-forming substances (e.g. honey, glue) are also found in the interior of bones.

4 Folds in skin are identical with folds in mountain ranges (apple).

5 Shrinkage folds in pollen caused by drying.

6 Bone structure (beak of the black stork) typical three-dimensional drawn nets, created by self-formation .

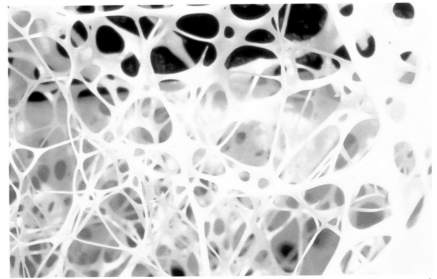

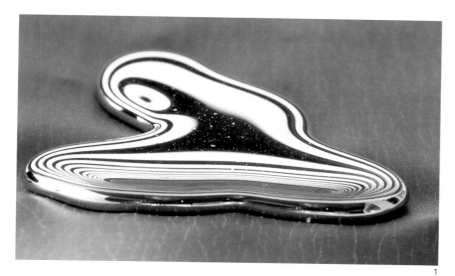

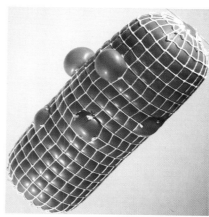

1 Equal surface tension in pneumatic constructions also allows deviations from spherical form (mercury).

2 Frozen soap bubble.
All pneumatic constructions can harden. The shells of crabs, sea urchins, crustaceans, nuts are hardened pneumatic constructions.

3 Model of a net pneumatic structure with typical bud formation.

Living Constructions, Models for Technology ?

Many artificial products are man's arms against the forces of nature. They are thus unnatural. This also includes houses and modern transport routes. Even man-made products that are formally identical with living objects remain artificial. Using natural materials does not make them natural either. Living creatures remain inimitable. Imitation of living constructions is worthwhile today at best in the manufacture of artificial limbs.

Man has learned from parents and teachers and man-made models. He has rarely imitated natural objects. They were and are motifs for art. In the meantime man has acquired more solid materials than are available in animate nature. He can build higher and across greater spans and move more rapidly than living objects. He has the wheel, the screw and machines. He is already concerned with machines that can think.

With the technical and artistic means at his disposal man is capable like no other living creature of developing countless new objects. He is thus extremely dangerous and can be extremely hostile to nature.

We have already become used to calling some constructions that seem less unnatural than others natural, biological or even ecological. This is misleading!

The high level of technology and science permits a more profound understanding of the natural than ever before. Among other things it makes it possible to mitigate the unnaturalness of many technologies and their products. It creates a basis for the use of man-made things as an aid for peaceful co-existence with other living creatures.

Experiments

Frei Otto developed models and methods in which forms generate themselves in order to observe and analyse the processes by which material objects originate in all realms of nature, technology and architecture. An enormous range of experiments were carried out at the IL as part of the basic research programme by various teams under the direction of Frei Otto. Here however only some of the models and experimental equipment are described that are used as form-finding methods in architectural design:

– soap film experiments to produce minimal areas as form-finding models for tension-loaded membrane and rope-network constructions;
– experimental apparatus to create pneumatically and hydraulically

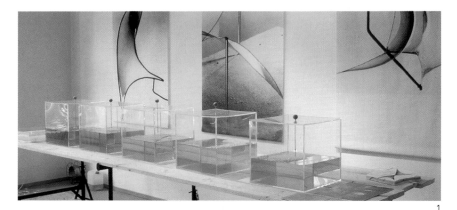

stressed membranes with rubber skins and other foils that harden after inflation;
– experiments with chains and chain-nets to find the form of suspended constructions stabilized by their own weight and for pressure-loaded vaults and lattice shells;

1 Apparatus for soap film experiments in the Villa Stuck, Munich, exhibition, 1992.

2 Apparatus for producing pneumatic constructions. Villa Stuck, Munich, 1992.

– experiments with plaster bandages to create pressure-loaded vault forms by the reversal of tension-loaded suspension forms;

– thread experiments to investigate branched constructions to find forms for optimized path systems;

– sand piles to create funnel forms and debris cones and to examine earth buildings and settlement constructions;

– experiments with tilting and rotating discs to investigate the stability of masonry constructions when tilted or in earthquakes;

– experiments with floating magnets to interpret surface occupation in urban development.

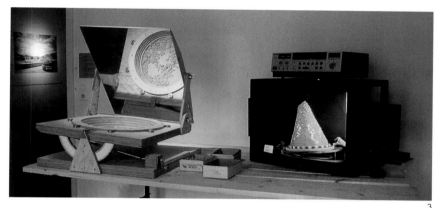

3

4

0,0 / 0,2

5

The models are essentially simple physical experiments that reveal the infinite diversity of possible forms and constructions without a great deal of effort. For example, these experiments made it possible to discover the hitherto entirely unknown structure forms like the rope loop or to explain the process by which cisterns originate.

The results of most of the experiments can now be recreated on the computer and made more precise if necessary.

Bodo Rasch's architectural practice develops numerical form-finding models based on the physical experiments devised by Frei Otto; the results are then used in the design process. Combining these programmes with current CAD software means that form-finding, statistical analysis, format and work planning can be done by computer.

In future it is certain that many numerical models will be developed with the aid of new computer algorithms based on fractal mathematics that can be used to analyse and simulate self-formation processes.

3 Tilting turntables to investigate the stability of masonry buildings. Villa Stuck, Munich, 1992.

4 Models made of plaster bandages. Villa Stuck, Munich, 1992.

5 Discharge funnel and spoil cone in dry sand.

Soap-film Experiments for Producing Minimal Surfaces

Membranes made up of liquids, known as "soap films", form when a closed frame is dipped into membrane-forming liquids and then taken out again. The frames can be made of thin wire or threads. The best-known membrane-forming liquid is soap lye. Very thin membranes are produced from distilled water with a few drops of detergent or "Pustefix" bubble fluid.

A membrane suspended in a frame has quite particular qualities. In a flat frame it is flat, in a non-flat frame it is in principle curved in a saddle shape.

A soap film always contracts to the smallest surface possible. It then takes up the form of the "minimal surface", which is clearly defined mathematically. Liquid membranes are under the same tension everywhere. They are prestressed, flexurally non-rigid and plane load-bearing constructions that are nevertheless tension loaded. The same is true of tents. The forms produced in the experiments – appropriately enlarged – can provide extremely precise models for the shape of tent constructions. Frei Otto used this analogy. This led to a new quality in tent-building architecture.

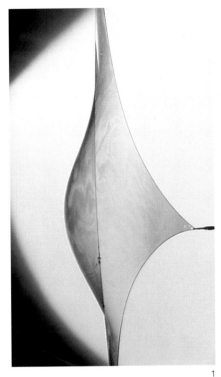

1

2

3

1   Soap film in wind tunnel.

2   Pointed tent soap film.

3   Soap film machine at the IL with soap film model in parallel light and camera.

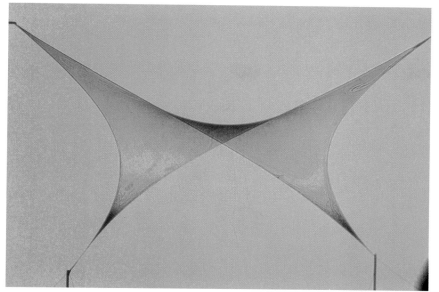

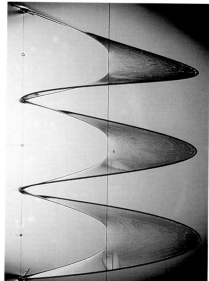

The soap film experiment can also be used to check whether the tension distribution in existing tents is largely optimal, by making the frame for the experiments as close to reality as possible. When tents deviate markedly from minimal area form this is obvious even to the unpractised eye. They do not just look wrong, they are also usually badly constructed as well.

A "soap film machine" was developed and built at the IL for the geometrical registration and measurement of soap film models: the soap film models can be preserved for longer in a climatic chamber. Parallel light is used to project the models in their real dimensions on to a photographic plate or a ground-glass screen; they are then photographed and measured. The forms produced in the soap film experiment are constructed as design and working models in the widest possible range of materials and used for further processing within the design process.

There are infinitely many different forms of soap films or minimal areas upon which membrane constructions of the most varied kinds – not just tents – can be modelled. The possibilities have by no means been exhausted. Fundamentally significant discoveries are still possible.

Frei Otto experimented at a very early stage when form-finding for membranes and nets for tent-like constructions with different membrane tensions. For this he used nets made of springs and rubber springs. A construction of this kind was used for an aircraft hangar.

4 Four-point sail soap film.

5 Soap film. Penetrating a spiral area with a flat plate.

6 Model of a soap film in a circle with vertical lamella.

Simple Experimental Apparatus to create the Form of Pneumatic Constructions

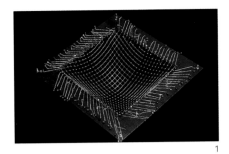

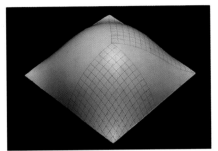

The apparatus for inflating clear transparent pneumatic constructions is a valuable aid, especially when finding forms for air-supported membrane halls. In this experiment a thin sheet of PVC or acrylic glass is heated and inflated with compressed air. The outline can be of any shape, and can be, for example, cut out of two sheets of plywood with a compass saw; the chosen plastic sheet is then placed between them and this package is then attached in a way in which it can be quickly removed to a base-plate with an opening for blowing in air. A battery of lamps placed over the experimental arrangement is used for heating. A powerful vacuum cleaner or hot-air fan is suitable to provide the blown air. After the form has been achieved the lamps are taken away and the inflated shape immediately sprayed with cold water and removed from the base-plate.

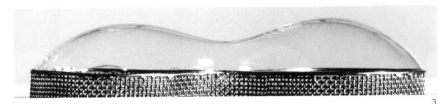

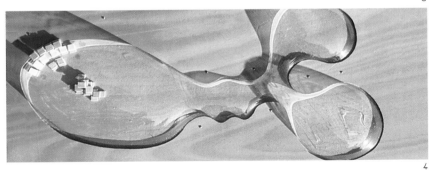

1, 2 Comparative examination of a pneumatically formed plaster model with a suspended net model.

3 Soap film on a dumb-bell plan. This produces two domes linked by a saddle.

4 Inflated acrylic shape. Project study for roofing a town in northern Canada with a transparent membrane.

Experiments with plastic-stiffened rubber films are also suitable for finding form for pneumatic constructions.

In this case rubber sheeting is used. It is inflated and placed on the glass fabric soaked in liquid polyester. Another method uses rubber films coated with liquid plaster. The rubber film is stretched over the underside of a sheet and fixed in a water-tight fashion in any desired outline. The film is filled and coated with freshly stirred liquid modelling plaster through a hole in the sheet. The plaster forms a skin and hardens. After about 45 minutes the model

5

can be turned round and the skin pulled off. This plaster-stabilized form is largely identical with a soap bubble in a frame of the same shape. This means that the membrane tensions in the rubber film are approximately the same in all directions. When an air hall is built in a similar shape on the basis of an experiment of this kind similar tensions in its membrane can be anticipated; they not only guarantee freedom from creasing but also make full use of the material. Of course further tests with larger air-supported models, static-dynamic calculations, wind tunnel experiments and others are necessary before an air hall is finally built. This model-building method is particularly suited for reaching a shape for air halls and water-filled membrane constructions. It also permits development by drawing of the final membrane made up of strips on the very precise plaster surface, which is then the "painting ground" for a spatially curved drawing.

5 The shapes in this plaster model are formed by reinforcing and articulating with ropes and nets and by anchoring at low points.

Experiments with Suspended Chains to find Shapes for Suspended Constructions

Suspended fine chains in a model precisely reproduce the form of ropes or wires suspended in the same way, in high-voltage cables, for example. A dense pattern of suspended chains gives the shape for suspended roofs that are stabilized by their own weight without pre-tension. Roofs of this kind are now found in large numbers all over the world. The shape of many of them was determined by chain models. It has long been known that the line described by a chain (hyperboloid cosine) can be seen as an idealized form of the free-standing arch or broad-span vault in stone or brick. Chain models reflect the arches and vaults that can be built with them as a model.

1

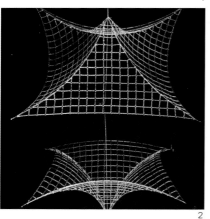

2

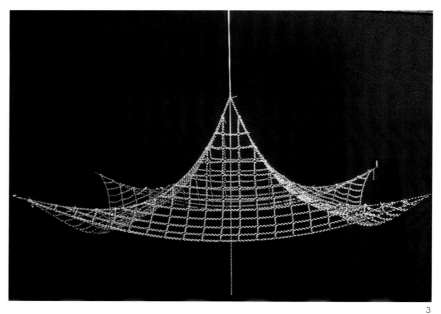

3

Chain networks showing significantly more complex forms than freely suspended individual chains can be constructed from small pieces of chain or short bars fastened together flexibly. Freely suspended networks of this kind open up the gigantic formal world of the "heavy tents", as the so-called gravity suspended roofs can also be named. They can be seen in the temple and pagoda roofs of the Far East, where they were originally made as flexible bamboo lattices. Today roofs of this kind are made of rope nets with a wooden or lightweight concrete roof.

1 Suspended model for the study of gravity suspended roofs.

2 Suspended model of a square-mesh suspended net made up of triangular segments and its reflection.

3 Suspended model using a square-mesh chain net shows the shape of Asian roofs.

Experiments for Producing Pressure-loaded Vault Forms by Reversing Tension-loaded Suspended Forms

Models made from medical plaster bandages are simple and easy to make, clear in their statement but only moderately accurate. They are dipped in water or sprayed with it and then hang like a soft skin; they then harden in a few minutes and retain their shape even when inverted.

Just as thread networks show the forms of lattice shells when they are taken from the suspended to the standing condition, in the same way the plaster bandages take the shape of shells with closed areas, first in the soft and then in the hardened condition. When dry the bandages are rigid, but very soft when wet. It is easy to establish that they do not produce "ideal" suspended forms if one sees that to mean that they cannot take compression forces in the suspended state. But all the forms found can be built on a larger scale, particularly in concrete or wood.

Other model methods (chain nets, loaded rubber films) and computer simulation can be used to capture the found forms more precisely. Experimentation with plaster bandages allows easy entry into form-finding work for shells, arches and vaults as roof, ceiling wall and bridge constructions, which in many cases can even be realized in unreinforced concrete or masonry, as there are no or very low tensile forces.

Suspended chain nets or nets made up of metal bars reflect "standing" curved rigid plane load-bearing constructions. They are lattice shells, also called net vaults, lattice domes or flexion-free shells. Nets made up of flexibly linked bars can become lattice shells when suspended by fixing the joints (e.g. soldering or gluing), and they are also particularly stable and bear well when standing.

Hundreds of different suspended net and shell forms have been examined by experiments of this kind as part of the work of Bodo Rasch, Frei Otto and the Institute for Lightweight Structure, and historic suspended roofs and vaults have also been interpreted.

Buildings have been erected in Germany (Multihalle Mannheim), Canada, the USA and Japan as constructions developed with chain nets and then used as lattice shells.

4, 5 Plaster bandage models are built suspended and inverted after drying.

6 Inversion of suspended shapes to find the shape of groin vaulting.

Sand Piles

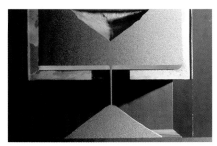
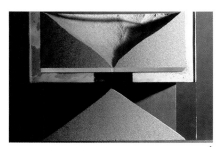

The shapes of volcanoes, screes in the mountains or mining spoil heaps are similar to each other. They belong to the formal canon of the spoil cone. When ramparts, dikes, groynes, spoil-, earth- and rubbish tips are being planned and constructed then knowledge about the self-formation process of spoil is an essential prerequisite. Any grainy material falling from a fixed point forms a cone on the surface below. If some of this granulate is released at one point then a funnel is formed within the granulate mass with the same angle of inclination, the "natural" angle of repose. The surface of a spoil cone or funnel with a natural angle of repose is relatively unstable. Vibration (earthquake, wind, rain, traffic) causes the spoil to slip or roll. This reduces the angle of repose, makes the slope more shallow and the earth construction more stable. The natural angle of repose plays a crucial part in civil engineering at or below ground level, in earth and foundation building and in garden design. If when excavating a road cutting for example the slope becomes steeper than the natural angle of repose then the surface is likely to slip if it is loosened by frost, heat or rain. There are infinitely many other forms alongside the geometrically very precise conical forms of spoil cones and funnels. All the forms created by spoil in nature and technology can be presented experimentally.

Suitable experimental materials are sand, fine gravel or chippings, but also salt, sugar and a number of other things. Forms of this kind can be created effortlessly with a very simple apparatus consisting of an upper and a lower plate arranged parallel to each other. The sand trickles through the holes in the upper plate and the funnel form appears at the top and underneath the spoil cone. Gentle vibration or inclination of the base plate makes the forms created flatter and thus more stable. The apparatus is useful for scientific investigation of natural constructions, e.g. for information about the earthquake stability of volcanoes, screes, dunes and hills. Experimental results from this apparatus are among the essential bases for design in earth, foundation and hydraulic engineering. As sand piles are also used in large-scale art (Land Art) the apparatus can also be used for artistic design.

1 Discharge funnels and spoil cones in dry sand.

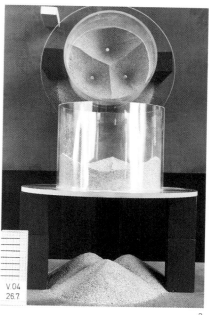

2

V.10
26.7.

3

V.04
26.7.

4

V.06
26.7.

5

6

2–4 The shape of discharge funnels and spoil cones depends on the arrangement and position of the holes.

5 Funnels and

6 spoil cones in an even layer of sand. The holes are arranged in a regular pattern.

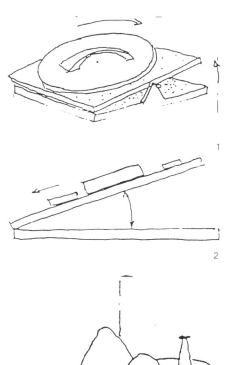

Experiments with Tilting and Turning Plates to examine the Stability of Brick and Stone Constructions

The stability of buildings can be investigated by placing a scale model on a turntable and then tilting and turning it. Stability against falling over is at its least in the direction in which the object is tipped. In the case of brick or masonry buildings it is possible to establish the danger of partial inner stability with the turntable if for example parts but not all of them collapse in the experiment. The apparatus is ideally suited to developing highly stable brick and stone constructions like walls, vaults, domes, arches and towers. It is also particularly suited to testing the stability of constructions that are particularly sensitive to earthquakes.

In an earthquake the ground under a building is severely accelerated and shifted laterally in a previously unknown direction. The inertial mass of the building causes the horizontal forces that occur, which are measured as a % of dead weight, and which attack every single element of the building. Stability against powerful earthquakes can be considered adequate if the model of a stone building does not collapse when the disc is tilted at an angle of 20–30%. This apparatus has confirmed previous insights about the threat to stone buildings from earthquakes, but has also provided new ones that make it possible to construct walls, towers, arches, vaults and domes that are stable and earthquake-proof.

1 Tilting turntables.

2 Plane tilted at 30°.

3 Tilting turntables with models.

4 Stability experiment on a dome with skylight. The photograph shows the construction shortly before it collapsed at a 40% inclination.

5 Stability experiments on a brick building with square ground plan, 1993.

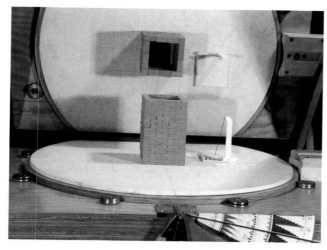
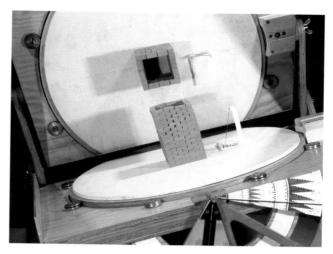

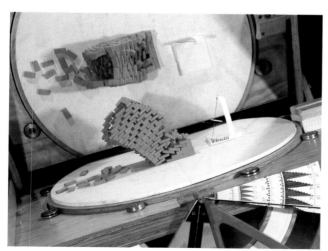
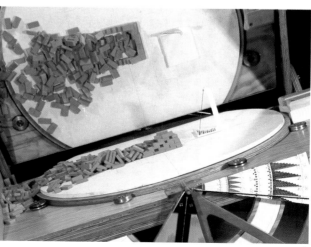

5

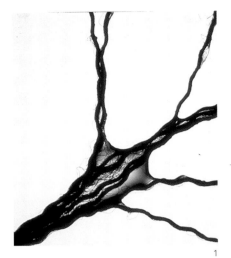

Experiments for the Investigation of Optimized Path Systems and Branched Constructions

In terms of model technology it is possible to represent the direct path system in which every traffic starting point is connected by a straight line to every destination with threads (e.g. rubber threads). From the traffic point of view the direct path system is ideal. There are no detours. But the overall path length and the area used for direct path systems is very large. The minimal path system is ideal for traffic routes (footpaths and cycle tracks, roads, railways, motorways) and a special experimental arrangement has been devised to investigate it. If the intention is to investigate the form of minimal requirement for the manufacture, maintenance and running of path systems and traffic then the model using moistened threads with "limited excess length" is particularly suitable. It can be considered a compromise between direct path system and minimal path system. Threads are stretched between the starting and terminus points for traffic. They indicate the direct path system. If the threads are loosened and given an excess length of 8%, for example, of the original length and the threads are then dipped into water (without detergents) then the threads are bundled by the surface tension of the water. In such configurations produced by bundling the "traffic paths" to be covered are 8% longer than in the direct path system but the area needed for the transport routes to be constructed and their overall length is significantly smaller. It is often only 30–50% of the direct path system. The "minimal detours" system aims at a minimum, in terms of the energy needed for the building and maintenance of the routes and for the traffic overall.

This very simple experimental procedure is also suitable for investigating power transport systems especially in lattice constructions made of compression- and bending-loaded slender bars. Here the convergences produce a slight extension of the power transport systems but also better use of materials because of shortening of effective length and free-span breadths. Typical branched constructions are created which under certain circumstances can be related to the appearance of deciduous trees. This very simple model construction method was developed by Frei Otto in 1958, refined in studies at Yale University in 1960 and brought to a highly developed level in many working stages, most recently by Marek Kolodziejczyk of Krakow at the Institute for Lightweight Structures and then in Atelier Warmbronn.

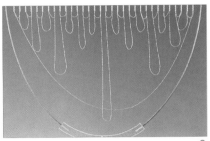

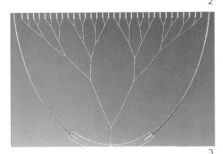

1 Macrophotograph of a thread model with water lamella and open branching.

Two-dimensional thread model to investigate a branched structure.

2 Free-hanging threads.

3 Bundled threads after dipping in water.

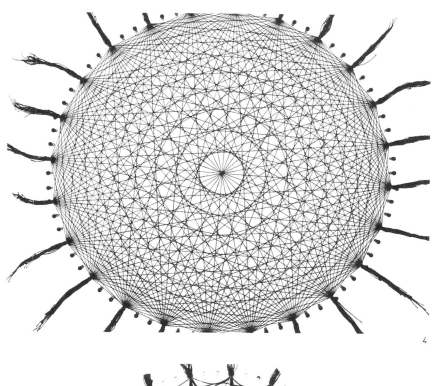

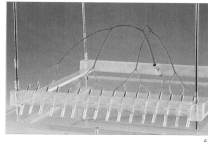

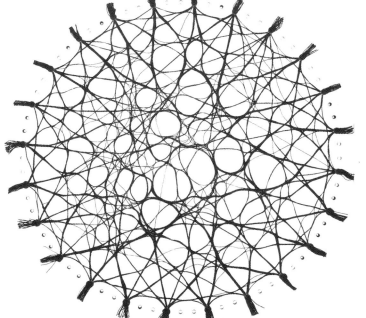

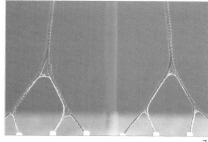

Two-dimensional thread model:

4 Direct path system, each point connected with all others.

5 Branched structure with closed mesh, a minimized detour system is produced after dipping in water.

6, 7 Three-dimensional thread model with open branches at the points of support. The model was built in suspension and turned over after drying.

All these models were built by Marek Kolodziejczyk at the IL.

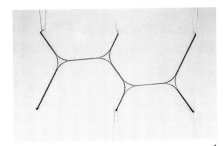

1

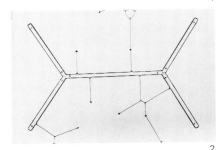

2

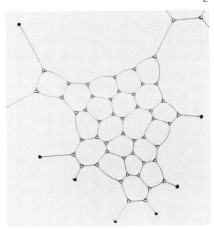

3

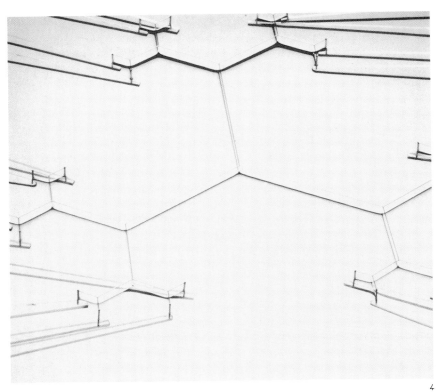

4

1 Minimal path system as soap lamellas between 6 points.

2 Minimal path system in two generations. Minimal path systems place themselves at a angle of 90° to a minimal path system built of fixed elements between 4 points.

3. Minimal path system with closed meshes.

4 Minimal path system as soap lamella between 24 points in the minimal path apparatus.

The so-called minimal path device can reliably determine a minimal path system between any number of points arranged in any number of ways in a matter of a few seconds. The key feature of the device is a sheet of glass placed precisely horizontally over a basin of water. It is sprayed with water from below. The water has a few drops of soap lye (detergent, Pustefix) mixed with it. The sheet of glass is touched with fine adjustable needles from below. The needles are fixed at the end of thin "fingers" that can be adjusted from the edge of the basin. If the water level is slowly lowered, films of soap form between the sheet of glass, the surface of the water and the needles. Soap films always shrink to the smallest possible surface area: the so-called minimal surface configuration. As the distance of the surface of the water to the underside of the glass is constant, the contact lines of the soap films on the under side of the glass plate have minimal overall length. These lines are visible from above. They can be measured photographically and read into electronic data storage systems. The apparatus was developed in 1958 in Atelier Frei Otto Berlin and has been used at the University of Stuttgart's Institute for Lightweight Structure since 1964.

Experiment for the Simulation of the Occupation of an Area

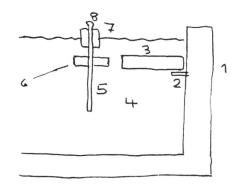

Many animals, including man, show territorial behaviour. They occupy areas that they defend as their own. If for example a very large area is settled by only one occupier (animal or human being) then the territory can be chosen at random. If there are two occupiers the territories move to the periphery, with the greatest possible distance between them. If there are many occupiers quite definite patterns are formed. The mechanisms of free area occupation can be observed on beaches, for example on lawns and in restaurants.

We are also familiar with "attracting" area occupation, when the occupiers move as close together as possible. This process is easily simulated using soap bubbles floating on the surface of water. The bubbles float together themselves and form thick packs with ground plans that are often hexagonal, but also pentagonal or heptagonal.

When working on urban development problems it is necessary to develop a procedure in which both repellent and attractive space occupation can be simulated at any density for any particular restricted area.

The outline form of the area to be occupied is cut out of perspex, for example, and placed in a shallow dish of water. Small bar magnets (magnetized pins, for example) held in a vertical position by floats are allowed to float in such a way that all the identical poles are either at the top or the bottom. The bar magnets repel each other and take up typical maximum distance positions. The positions are reached by the magnets "of their own accord" by several "occupiers" in the middle of the field precisely to the millimetre without outside aid. More powerful magnets or bundles of magnets have larger "territories" than weaker or individual magnets.

This experimental approach also makes it possible to simulate attracting combined with repellent occupation, of the kind that can be observed for example in groups of people in village communities, who move close together for economic or security reasons but keep their distance from other groups. In this case the attracting occupations are achieved by repolarizing some of the magnets so that the unlike poles attract each other.

Paths appropriate for optimized path systems and branching constructions can be determined by this experimental approach and the configurations that it produces.

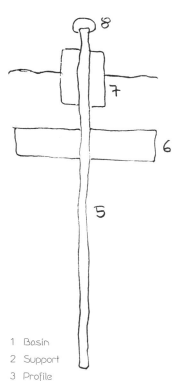

1 Basin
2 Support
3 Profile
4 Water
5 Magnetized needle
6 Round disc
7 Float (e.g. Polystyrene foam)
8 Luminous head

Sketch of model structure for area occupation simulation apparatus.

Tent Structures

Tents are among man's oldest built constructions. They have been used as accommodation in many cultures for millennia. Tents with various forms, constructions and equipment came into being according to the available materials, climatic conditions and social constructions. Continuous development through all stages of history brought about an optimization of this structure, as can be seen from Bedouin tents, the Asian yurt (1), the North American tepee and also the European circus tent. "Classical" forms have developed within an art of tent-making that has matured empirically and in terms of craft.

Tents are stretched plane load-bearing constructions made of sheeting, woven fabric or nets. The structure consists of one or more compression-stressed supports and tension-loaded membranes. Tent construction research after 1950, Frei Otto's research and development work, started a new overall view of this structural form. Frei Otto was the first to examine the link between form and structure and thus discovered the significance of the self-forming minimal surface for the design and shape of tent structures.

Minimal surfaces are saddle-shaped curved formations with the smallest possible area within a closed periphery. Tent skins, whose form corresponds to the minimal area, are stretched equally in all directions. They are subject to their own formal canon and scarcely at all to the arbitrariness of the designer. Form and structure make up an indivisible unity of unmistakable form.

Frei Otto invented and developed models and methods in which correct tent forms are produced by self-formation: minimal surfaces are produced experimentally in a simple way with membrane-forming liquids (soap lye). The shape then produces itself with the prescribed periphery and shows, appropriately enlarged, the shape of the membrane or the net in the building.

The following tent types can be distinguished according to their formal elements: the simple sail (6) is an edge supported tent. Forces are introduced by peripheral ropes into the supports at upper and lower points.

The pointed tent is supported at one point and the forces are distributed via rope- or strap-reinforced grooves and ribs, via a rope loop, the so-called eye, or via the "garland" (several accumulated eyes).

The arched tent has linear support from a compression-loaded arch; thus the membrane stabilizes the arch and stops it from collapsing.

The humped tent is supported two-dimensionally, the forces are distributed homogeneously (supports with lamellas, mushroom-

1 Kirghiz yurt, a structure with a wooden lattice wall and a barred domed covered with heat-insulating blankets and cloths.

2 North American Indian tepee.

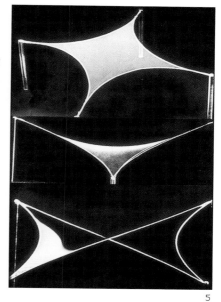

5

6

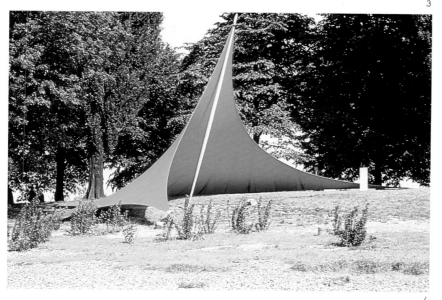

4

3 A group of pointed tents roofed the Swiss pavilion at the Lausanne district exhibition.

4 The small pavilion at the Federal Garden Exhibition in Cologne, 1957, is a mixture of sail and pointed tent.

5 Soap film of a four-point sail.

6 The four-point sail was pitched between two high and two low points as a music pavilion at the Federal Garden Exhibition in Kassel in 1955.

shaped supports) or via individual points (branched support, individual bracing).

The wave tent is a peripherally supported membrane whose surface forms parallel or stellar waves. There are any number of hybrid forms as well as these standard types.

Form-shaping elements can also be investigated by self-generating form-finding processes and integrated into the formation process of the minimal area in soap film experiments.

The shapes of all Frei Otto's and Bodo Rasch's tent constructions can be created with soap film models. Other model building methods are also used when seeking shapes; these involve the thinnest possible rubber films, the finest possible knitted and woven fabrics, tulle, thread or wire nets.

The physical model of equal tension is also simulated by the computer. "Finite element" calculation methods are usually used in such cases. This produces idealized forms that can be processed by the computer until the final planning stages. All constructions built by Frei Otto and Bodo Rasch after 1970 were computer generated and drawn – without rejecting the striking physical model. Computer simulation was first introduced by Klaus Linkwitz in 1966, on Frei Otto's suggestion.

Frei Otto's research and development work was made accessible to a broader public by the publication of his dissertation "Das hängende Dach" (The suspended roof) in 1954. The fundamental principles, pointing the way forward were as ever translated into the realm of architecture in the tent constructions that he designed with Peter Stromeyer for the Garden Exhibition in Kassel (1955), Cologne (1957) and Hamburg (1963). The constructions used for pavilions and exhibition areas count as "classical tents". They could not be more beautiful in terms of form, nor improved upon in their use of materials and load-bearing capacity.

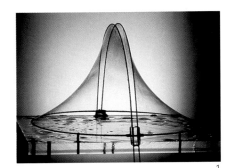

1

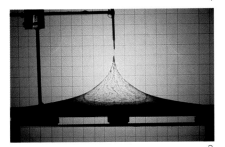

2

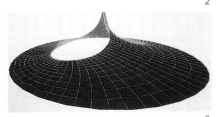

3

1 Soap film model of an arch-supported membrane.

2 Soap-film model of a membrane surface with rope loop as its high point.

3 Computer simulation of a minimal surface with rope loop.

4

4 Night photograph of the great wave hall at the International Garden Exhibition in Hamburg, 1963.

5 Soap film model of a parallel wave tent.

5

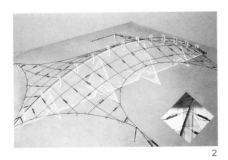

The entrance to the 1957 Federal Garden Exhibition in Cologne was spanned by an arch-supported membrane construction, the so-called "entrance arch"; it was visible over a considerable distance as the "gateway" to this show (1). Stabilization by a prestressed membrane means that the compression-stressed arch can be made very thin. The entrance arch spanned an area 34 m long and 24 m wide with a tube diameter of 17 cm (wall thickness 1.4 cm). A translucent fibre-glass fabric was used as a tenting membrane for the first time. Two small pavilions, a humped tent (4) and a pointed tent (p. 75, 4) were placed on the banks of the Rhine as protection from the rain.

The humped tent, a membrane structure with two humps over two masts, spanned 180 sqm. The branched support heads with 19 ribs were developed in self-generating form finding processes and achieve equal tension throughout the tent.

1 The entrance to the 1957 Federal Garden Exhibition in Cologne was spanned by the so-called entrance arch.

2 Form-finding model in steel wire and spring net for the Cologne entrance arch.

3 The entrance arch at night.

4

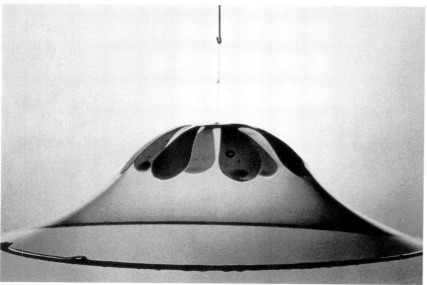

5

6

4 Small pavilion consisting of a double-humped membrane on the bank of the Rhine at the 1957 Federal Garden Exhibition in Cologne.

5 Soap film, distorted into a so-called hump with elastic lamellas.

6 Support for the humped tent in Cologne was by two branched posts.

The star-shaped tent covered a 684 sqm dance floor surrounded by, the so-called dance fountain (4). Alternating mast-supported high points and freely guyed low points create a reference to the surrounding landscape on all sides. The balanced up and down movement of the periphery and the lightness of the structure make the roof seem to float above the fountains. The wavy star shape corresponds to the light-hearted charm of the place and symbolizes the movement of dancing.

The shape of the stellar wave corresponds to the minimal area produced in the soap film model. The form and arrangement of the six steel lattice masts is reduced to the minimum necessary to transfer the forces. The tent is still standing, although it was planned for a single summer. The cotton sailcloth has been replaced by a polyester fabric. The "Tanzbrunnen" has become a popular institution and it is hard to imagine Cologne without it.

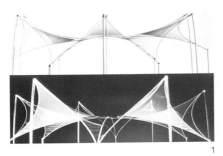

1

2

3

1 The soap film model for the Dance Fountain in Cologne.

2 The shape for the Thowal star-wave tent was computer generated

3 and tested as a tulle model.

4 The membrane for the Cologne Dance Fountain was originally made of cotton and later replaced with polyester fabric.

5 The Thowal star wave was built as a purely fabric structure because its span was so small.

In 1991 Bodo Rasch and his team had the opportunity of realizing one of Frei Otto's "classical" tents with more highly developed technology for a beach palace in Saudi Arabia. With the assistance of Frei Otto, the tent constructions for this palace complex were planned, manufactured, dispatched and erected in the incredibly short time of three months. Extreme care in detail planning made a technical optimum possible. Both the determination of shape and cut were developed on the computer and then tested and refined using several tulle models.

In the private area of the beach residence a stellar wave tent (5) shades the garden terrace used by the immediate family. As the structure had such a narrow span covering and area of 150 sqm this tent could be built as a pure textile structure. Belts in high-performance polyester fabric were used instead of steel ropes for the ribs, grooves and edges. They were set in hems and thus protected from solar UV radiation.

Belts and membranes are so mutually adjusted in terms of stretching that all components of the structure behave similarly in terms of elasticity. This means that details can be highly integrated and minimized. As well as this, pure textile constructions present considerable advantages in erection, stretching and the structure's behaviour under extreme loads.

4

5

1 The cross-wave tent membranes were made of cotton fabric.

2 Adding five high wave elements together produced the great wave hall at the International Garden Exhibition in Hamburg, 1963.

3 The five-axis wave tent in Thowal was tailored from PVC-coated polyester fabric, 1991.

Frei Otto built wave tents in cotton fabric as exhibition pavilions and halls for the 1963 garden exhibition in Hamburg. Their purity of form had a sculptural character in its balance of lightness and elegance (1, 2). The structural system for the four cross-wave tents (1), which covered exhibition areas of 125 sqm (15 m x 15 m) in each case, corresponds to a star wave with four high and four low points. The high points are supported by lattice masts, the low points guyed off. The cotton fabric membranes were reinforced at the mastheads in order to take up concentrations of tension.

The assembly tent for the beach palace in Thowal covers a circular assembly area of 700 sqm and serves as a reception tent for official guests. The lucid, austere form of the five-axis, centrally symmetrical tent is appropriate for its prestigious task without becoming paralysed in formal order references (3). Corner points taken down to ground level define the interior space and upward-curving edges pointing outwards provide access and exterior views. Apertures in the membrane at the mastheads admit air and light. All parts were made of stainless steel to stand up to the demands of the maritime climate. The membranes were tailored in PVC-coated polyester fabric with a fluoride cover coating.

A membrane awning with five high and four low points covers the spectators' stand on the beach residence sports field. Problems about roofing stands in larger stadia were also studied from this

1

3

relatively small roof (180 sq m) and solutions in principle sought. To give the spectators an open view of the playing field the front of the awning is supported by a broadly-spanned arc of rope along its whole length. The membranes find their curved, stable shape through the alternating high and low points of the rear edge. The awning itself, again a pure fabric structure, is made of PVC-coated polyester fabric, reinforced at the edges with polyester belts. A strap garland provides the connection to the peripheral arc rope. Frei Otto designed two tents of similar size for special occasions for Queen Elizabeth II, the festival tent at Dyce near Aberdeen in Scotland (5) and a design that was not realized for a festival tent on the Shetland island of Sullom Voe (4). Both constructions were designed for frequent pitching and striking, like circus tents. The

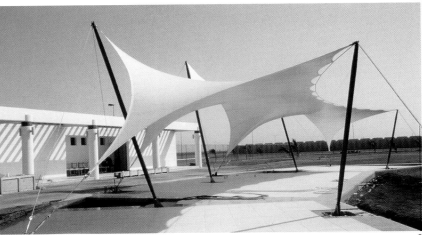

1-3 The membrane awning over the stand at the Thowal sports field was built in 1991 as a pure fabric structure.

Aberdeen tent (later pitched in London's Hyde Park) covered an area of 3300 sq m, and the membrane was distorted to provide stability by hump supports and low points. In contrast, the plan for the Sullom Voe tent was to stretch the tent fabric over an area of 40 m by 80 m with guys suspended from masts. This is a simple solution, and particularly stormproof. The materials intended for both constructions are the same: membranes in polyester-reinforced cotton, masts and guys in hot-galvanized steel.

4

5

6

4 Lamella support for the humped tent at Dyce near Aberdeen, 1975.

5 Design model for Elizabeth II's festival tent in Sullom Voe, 1981.

6 Interior view of the humped tent pitched in Aberdeen and later in Hyde Park.

1

2

3

4

1, 2 The Sarabhai tent developed in 1973 can be extended to cover any desired area.

3 The tent with snow at the IL.

4 The Sarabhai tent photographed while cutting the outer walls.

Frei Otto developed a very flexible frame tent, the Sarabhai tent, named after the clients Gautham and Gira Sarabhai, India. The tubular aluminium and sailcloth structure covers an area of 4 m by 4 m. The single tent was conceived as a unit to which additions can be made so that areas of any size can be roofed.

Colourfully painted and ornamented tents are known from historical and native examples. The study model of a painted tent was designed in the Warmbronn studio in 1985 as a contribution to "Golden Eye", an joint India–United States venture whose aim was to manufacture craft products designed by invited architects and designers in India and exhibit and sell them in the USA. The results were exhibited in the Cooper-Hewitt Museum in New York in 1985. The membrane structure is centrally supported by a tree-support which makes it possible to round off the top of the tent and thus no cutting of the fabric is necessary.

5

6

7

5 View of the design model for the pavilion with branched support, 1985.

6 View from below.

7 The painted round tent (contribution to "Golden Eye") was made and painted in India to an Atelier Warmbronn design. The light rattan frame is constructed in such a way that it can be put up like an umbrella. The cotton fabric covering was painted before sewing with decoration borrowed from traditional Indian motifs.

1

The coloured pointed tent, the so-called Heart Tent, is the "heart" of the Gardens of the Riyadh Diplomatic Club. The structure consists of a supporting rope network and a covering of hand-painted sheets of 8 mm thick safety glass. The ten segments, each consisting of 200 individual sheets, were each painted in a particular basic colour and complement each other in a finely graded play of colour. Bettina Otto's designs for the painting were developed with the aid of various models and the painting was executed in various stages in UV-resistant paints by the artist herself.

The garden with exotic plants, palm groves, fountains and pools forms a green oasis amidst the bleak desert and mountain landscape. It is surrounded by a curved band of masonry walls in natural stone that links the spaces in this palace-like complex. Three large membrane constructions join up with the outer wall and form a space for receptions, conferences and celebrations. The stark contrast between the heavy linear element of the walls and the light, bright membrane halls creates a fascinating spatial diversity.

2

1-3 Heart Tent, designed and painted by Bettina Otto, 1988.

3

Diplomatic Club in Riyadh, Saudi Arabia, 1988:

1 The enclosing walls were built of Riyadh sandstone and the tents tailored in fibre-glass fabric.

2 The whole Diplomatic Club complex, now known as the Tuwaiq Palace.

3 View from below into the semicircular window that forms the upper conclusion of the membrane and the combining element for connection with the wall.

2

1

3

Net Constructions

Rope net constructions are subject to the same laws as membrane tent constructions, but they can cover considerably larger spans.

Single-sided and double-sided (saddle-shaped) curved surfaces can be formed with even-meshed nets if the angles of the net ropes can change at the node. A net is usually manufactured flat and acquires its final, spatially curved shape by pre-tension in the fitting process. Frei Otto built his first large tent with Peter Stromeyer for the Swiss "Neige et Rocs" pavilion (2/3) at the 1963 Swiss National Exhibition in Lausanne. The 36 m span of the tent group was so large that normal tent cloth could not be used. The project had to be finished under considerable time pressure and so a reinforcement for the cotton fabric was improvised by the simple device of fastening a net of PVC-coated ropes immediately underneath the membrane. Here the membrane was also an aid to cutting out, because every mesh of the net had been precisely determined earlier in the development. As an intermediate stage the structure clearly illustrates the transition from pure membrane construction to rope net construction.

Frei Otto undertook fundamental research in parallel with the project work. His team studied examples of net constructions in nature and technology, carried out experiments in form determination and developed new model building methods. An important result of this work was the development of a standard net that can be quickly prefabricated and used for most spans.

The net was conceived in such a way that it can be prefabricated by machine, assembled either in the air or on the ground and raised on masts. As the chosen width for the mesh is 50 cm a human being cannot fall through it, and so no scaffolding is needed when it is being put up. Mechanical prefabrication of the net in strips guarantees quick assembly and easy transportation. A roof skin can be hung or stretched under or over the net as a protection against the weather. Rope thicknesses of 8, 12 and 16 cm with rope clamps as connecting- and end-nodes were to be used. At this stage in development an opportunity arose to translate the results into building practice. The competition for the German pavilion in Montreal was announced in 1965. The design submitted by Rolf Gutbrod and Frei Otto of a rope net construction as a roof for the pavilion won first prize and was realized in association with Peter Stromeyer.

Only 13 months passed between planning the building and completion of the spatial covering. The simple manufacture of the net, the ease with which it could be installed and above all the safety of erection attracted attention from all over the world.

1, 2 The membrane for the "Neige et Rocs" pavilion in Lausanne in 1963 was reinforced with net of ropes.

3 This model is part of several form-finding studies for the support of textile membranes and rope nets and gave Frei Otto and Rolf Gutbrod the design idea for the German pavilion at the 1967 Montreal World Fair.

4 The net for the experimental structure and later the building for the Institut for Lightweight Structures, was assembled from prefabricated strips.

3

4

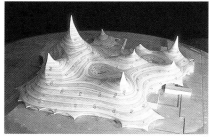

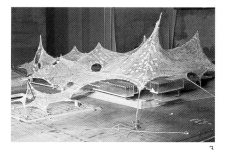

The net was made up of steel ropes 12 mm thick with a mesh width of 50 cm. It was made up in 15 m wide strips in Konstanz (L. Stromeyer und Co.) and shipped to Montreal in rolls. Despite strict North American safety regulations assembly in the air was completed without a safety net or scaffolding while work proceeded underneath.

The rope net construction had eight high and three low attachment points, was supported by masts between 14 and 36 m in height and covered an overall area of about 8,000 sqm. A membrane of PVC-coated Polyester fabric was suspended 50 cm below the net as protection against the weather. The pavilion was planned to stand for two years, but the construction was actually not taken down until six years later, when the site was needed for the Olympic regatta.

Numerous models were built to investigate the form and cut of this rope net construction: soap film models, form study models and demonstration models in tulle, measurement models in wire and experimental models in wood. The forces in the net wires were tested on a steel wire model at a scale of 1:75 using measuring devices specially developed for the purpose by Eberhard Haug and Frei Otto in the IL.

Wherever possible, Frei Otto tries to design the most important details of buildings entrusted to him in such a way that they will

1 The large measurement model for the German pavilion in Montreal was built to a scale of 1:75 and served to establish the ultimate form and to investigate support performance.

fulfil the needs of the construction and the task in hand with a minimum of materials. The rope net clamps intended as net nodes for the Montreal net were developed with this in mind: the so-called cross-clamp had to be light and free of corners and edges so as to make it easier to roll and unroll the strips of netting. The clamps were placed 50 cm apart on ropes 12 mm in diameter.

This system proved to be particularly easy to assemble and reasonable in price, and additionally permits striking without damage and re-use of the ropes and clamps. It was used as a connection system in several large buildings.

The construction of the exhibition areas, which were placed freely in the space, was also conceived by Frei Otto. For deadline reasons the prefabricated, galvanised steel parts for the construction had to be ordered before the design for the interior space was complete. A multi-stage system had been developed whose individual elements for ceiling loads of about 6 kN/sqm had been reduced to what was absolutely necessary for force transmission. Rapid assembly, low ceiling height and adequate spans (a maximum of 7 fields of 1.25 m system length) were the

4

2 A layer-line wooden model was built for wind tunnel experiments.

3 The tulle demonstration model shows the whole pavilion.

4 The cross clamp was developed by Frei Otto for the Montreal net in 1967.

5 Partial view of the pavilion with the inserted terrace constructions.

5

principal conditions. The system was conceived for free adaptation to the exhibition in such a way that the vertical supports are not attached at definite points and so the exhibition was not restricted by the placing of the supports. The supporting elements are adjusted to the different loads produced by the irregular placing of supports by division into upper and lower belts.

1

1   The net for the pavilion in position.

2   Overall view of the completed building. The pavilion was built according to Frei Otto's and Rolf Gutbrod's competition design in 1967.

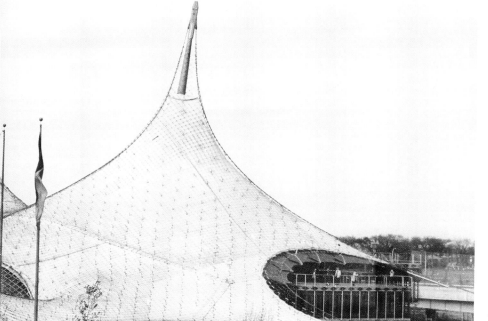

3 A membrane of PVC-coated Polyester fabric was suspended 50 cm under the net to form a roof skin.

4 Model of the inserted terrace construction with support head.

5 Interior view of a low point with eye. In the window areas a membrane of flexibly connected, transparent sheets was combined with the roof skin. This detail was the prototype of the roof skin of the Olympic roof in Munich, for which the pre-stressed sheets of acrylic glass were combined with soft plastic profiles.

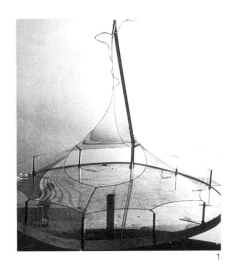

An experimental structure was erected on the university campus in Stuttgart-Vaihingen in 1966 to test the construction and assembly of the Montreal pavilion. Frei Otto had fixed the size of this experimental structure (460 sqm of roofed area) at a seventeenth of the area of the Montreal pavilion with the intention of using the net later as a support system for the Institute for lightweight structures (IL), which he had founded in 1964.

The construction of the anticlastically curved roof is reduced to that which is absolutely necessary. It consists of the tensile-loaded steel net with equal mesh; the compression-loaded steel tubular mast as an articulated support; the flexible, tensile-loaded edge; and 12 guying points, again divided into pressure- and tensile-loaded components.

The net has a mesh width of 50 cm and had been prefabricated in four strips which were then fitted together to form two symmetrical sections on site and suspended within the peripheral ropes. The tubular steel mast was raised by a crane and temporarily guyed with ropes. The ridge and eye edge cables were fastened to the masthead and the net was drawn evenly and slowly up the mast. The peripheral cables were fixed into the anchorage points and the net suspended in the ridge and eye edge cables. Pre-tension in the net was achieved by hydraulic raising of the mast and tension on the anchorage points. The sand-tub in which the mast was mounted was filled with sand to fix it in position.

1 The soap film model for the experimental structure and later institute building shows the minimum surface within the prescribed periphery.

2 Double exposure of the wire model shows deformation in the net under load.

3 A roof skin was suspended 50 cm under the net to test the membrane suspensions.

4 The mast is raised by a crane and then temporarily guyed with cables.

5 The net, assembled from 4 strips, is suspended on cables on ridges or the eye edges.

6 The completed net structure for the experimental building.

2

1

After standing for two years the experimental building was dismantled, re-erected 2km away and extended for use as the home of the Institut for Lightweight Structures:

The net was removed, folded from the edge, wrapped around the mast and transported by crane to the new site. There it was pitched again within a day. Subsequently the roof was covered and the interior closed off with an all-round glass facade and extended as a room for the institute.

The institute building is one of the few tents in long-term use and occupies an important and unique place in Frei Otto's work and in 20th century architecture. Research and teaching have been conducted under the roof for 25 years. It has become famous as a forum and cradle for light-weight building under Frei Otto's direction, and has provided space for seminars, conferences and large celebrations with participants from all over the world.

1 For transport to the new site the net was loosened, folded from the edge and wrapped round the mast.

2 The net was put up again at the new site using the same method.

3 Putting on the support laths for the first timber covering.

4 View of the roof of the Institute for Lightweight Structure on the Stuttgart University campus at Vaihingen.

5 (Page 104) Interior views of the institute.

6 (Page 105) The listed building was renovated in 1993. The roofing, flooring, facade glazing and the window opening in the roof ('eye') were renewed. Planning and site direction were undertaken by Bodo Rasch's architectural office.

Early in 1968 Frei Otto was commissioned to make it possible to build the constructions suggested by Behnisch und Partner in their entry for the competition for the Olympic roofs in Munich. Behnisch's design was modelled on the rope structure of the German pavilion in Montreal, and could therefore be realized only with Frei Otto and his team's involvement. Frei Otto built a large number of pre-design and detail models and carried out building feasibility tests. The final decision to build was made in May 1968 on the basis of the tulle model (3) of the whole project, although some design changes were made after this.

Olympic roofs in Munich, 1972:

1 Interior view of the stadium roof. The net has a mesh width of 75 cm and was covered with sheets of acrylic glass.

2 View.

3 Tulle design and demonstration model.

While work was in hand on these constructions, new methods of mathematical and geodetic calculation, complementing model building, were developed at the IL.

Measurement models at a scale of 1:125 were designed according to the engineers' preliminary calculations of forces in net, supports and guys, and from geometrical data from the design models, calculated in detail and model-statically. The forces and strains measured in the measurement model were translated directly according to scale. They were used to find form dependent upon the overall support behaviour with the desired surface tensions, support and anchorage forces, and the loads and strain resulting from these for the load cases of self-weight, snow and wind.

4

The forces in the individual net wires (every 4th cable was represented) were measured mechanically between two net nodes, first with the redeveloped Montreal measuring device, then later with dial gauges also developed in the IL by Jürgen Hennicke and Frei Otto.

The models were measured photogrammetrically and with the aid of a three-dimensional measuring bench that recorded the spatial situation of selected areas in co-ordinates. Several fixed Linhof cameras were used to take double-exposed photographs of the loaded and the unloaded state. From these photographs the strains caused by the added load could be established.

7

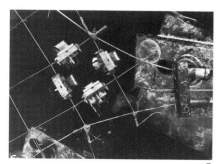

5

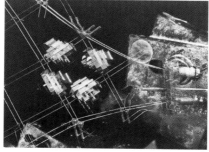

6

4 The large measurement model for the stadium roof. The models were built by Frei Otto and his team at the Institute for Leightweight Structures.

5 Net edge of the measurement model with suspended dial gauges.

6 Double exposure shows the deformation of the net wires under load.

7 Detail of the measurement model. Net edge.

1

2

3

The net for the aviary in the zoo at Munich-Hellabrunn covers like a delicate, scarcely visible veil a mature meadow landscape with large, old trees on the banks of a stream. The character of the net also changes according to the season and the incidence of light; it fits in with its surroundings like a part of nature.

The net has a very fine mesh width of 60 x 60 mm and spans a large, high interior of 4,600 sqm, in which about 20 different species of bird can fly freely. It is supported by 10 masts and is suspended on mobile clamping plates.

The net was made of stainless steel wire 3.5 mm thick and is calculated to withstand a maximum snow load of 35 kg/m². The net has a breaking load of 22 t/m. It was welded together from strips on the ground, raised on the masts and then arranged in its ultimate shape. The gaps needed for the trees during fitting were subsequently closed .

1 The tulle design model shows the whole aviary in the zoo at Munich-Hellabrunn.

2 The single low point of the scarcely visible aviary net.

3 The aviary was built in 1979/80 to a design by Jörg Gribl and Frei Otto.

4 View of the aviary net shimmering in the sunlight.

4

1 The sports hall in Jeddah was built on the basis of this design model in fine brass chains.

2 Interior of the hall.

3 Exterior view of the completed hall.

4 Interior view of the hall under construction without internal membrane.

The support structure for the sports hall in Jeddah, completed in 1980, is a rope net construction similar to the net in Montreal. The shape of the roof was arrived at by using a soap film model. The first design model in fine brass chains (1) showed the construction originally intended, a suspended rope net roof with wooden members and a shingle covering. The final shape was fixed using a fine Polyester silk model showing how the hall would be integrated into the surrounding development. The roof covers the sport and spectator area and covers an arena of 7,500 m² (max. size 110m x 80m). Eight tubular steel masts up to 30 m high support the even-meshed steel rope net, which is covered with an outer and an inner membrane.

building industry but to put a protective covering like a plastic bag from the packaging industry over the aerial and then inflate it. This had the additional advantage that no small metal parts would interfere with the ultra-short wave reception. The first Radom was inflated in about 1954. Walter Bird set up his own firm "Birdair" which soon became a world leader in the manufacture of air halls and ultimately of tents with poles as well.

At almost the same time as Walter Bird, but at first without knowing him, Frei Otto was pushing forward; he was working on inflating aluminium membranes as early as 1952 (literature: Das hängende Dach). He developed and built tents for Stromeyer Zelte and observed that pole-supported tents can stand without poles if there is increased interior pressure (e.g. exterior wind suction). He concluded from this that it is possible to do without poles if the

3

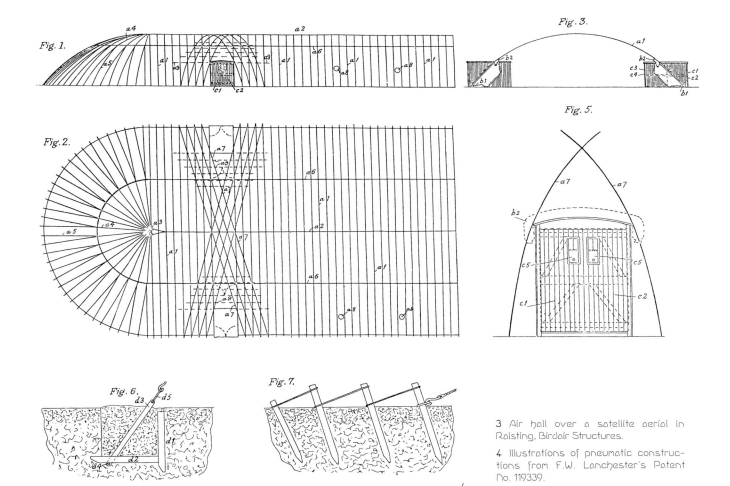

3 Air hall over a satellite aerial in Raisting, Birdair Structures.

4 Illustrations of pneumatic constructions from F.W. Lanchester's Patent No. 119339.

4

interior pressure is maintained by wind suction, or by fans when there is no wind. his first suggestions for wind-supported tents date from 1956/57. he planned the first air-supported tent for a factory with three domes each 800 m in diameter (literature: C. Roland, 'Frei Otto, Spannweiten'). The second suggestion was for a Stromeyer project, an exhibition pavilion for the 1958 Floriade in Rotterdam, but this was not built.

1958-61 saw intensive basic research by Frei Otto and his colleagues Siegfried Lohs, Dieter Frank and Ewald Bubner, in close co-operation with mathematician and structural engineer Rudolf Trostel. The key work "Zugbeanspruchte Konstruktionen Band I" (Tension-loaded Structures volume I) was produced, in which considerable space was devoted to pneumatically tensioned membrane constructions. This book, which appeared in 1962, contains projects and ideas for almost all the pneumatic

1 Industrial plant with three pneumatically supported domes, design 1958.

2 Design for a spherical pneumatic structure as a bulk material store.

3 Exhibition pavilion for the 1958 Floriade in Rotterdam. In this design a pneumatic structure is reinforced with a rope net with hexagonal mesh.

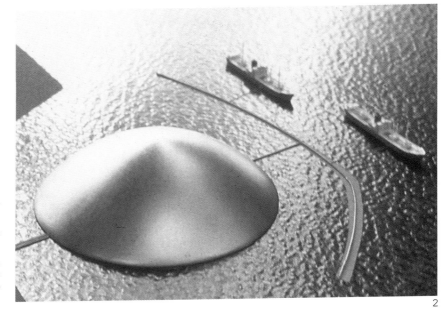

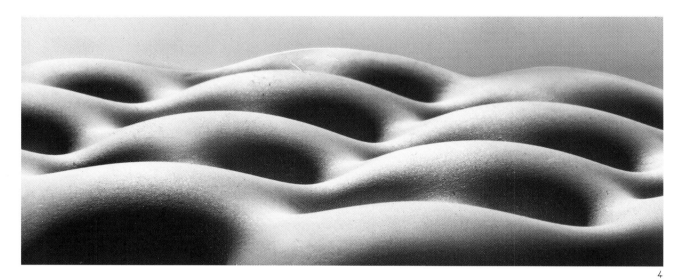

constructions known today – square, rectangular, indeed with any ground plan, also floating, as greenhouses or baths, with interior drainage, for unrestrictedly large areas, e.g. for the roofing of estates, and also for water– and earth–filled pneumatic constructions for dams, disaster protection, and many more.

The subsequent period was governed by practice rather than developments and inventions. Architects and engineers in the United States, Germany, England, France and Japan built, within a brief period, about 20 000 warehouses, sports facilities (especially swimming baths, indoor tennis courts, stadium roofs), greenhouses and exhibition buildings. Building was undertaken, with the exception of a small number of serious projects, without basic knowledge and at first without including the pioneers. There were many losses in severe storms, for example, in 1968 a single

4 Shape study for an air hall with internal drainage. Plaster model.

5 Plaster model of a pneumatic structure tied in crosswise.

6 Soap bubble model tied in crosswise.

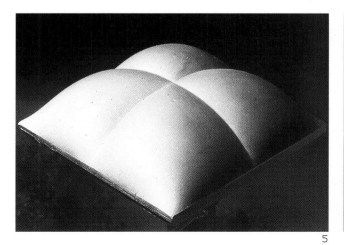

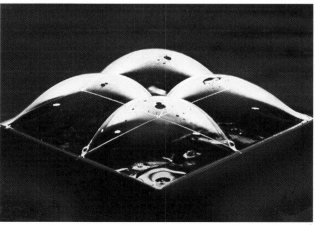

5

6

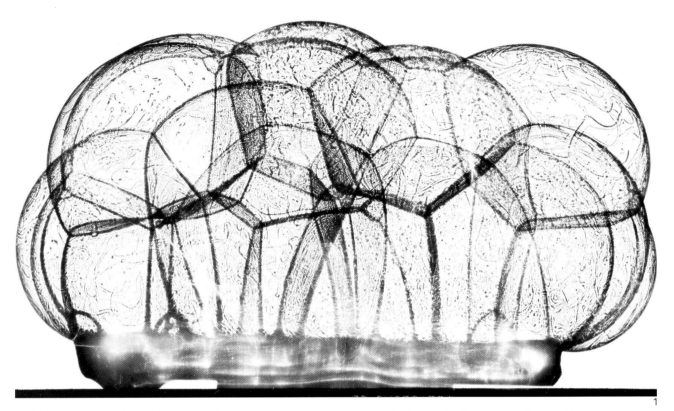

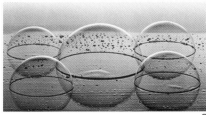

storm blew down about 200 air halls in northern Europe. Some were destroyed by heavy snowfalls, when electricity for the fans failed or snow blocked the air inlets.

But the halls were improved step by step. Large capacity air halls were built even in the most difficult climates. Ideas for building large rope nets under which residential and working space could be created in inhospitable areas which had already been sketched out in "Das hängende Dach" were taken up and brought closer to realization with the aid of the air hall.

1 Soap bubbles, foam structure.

2 Large central bubble surrounded by four independent small bubbles.

3 "Penta-dome" exhibition pavilion, 1958.

4

5

The US pavilion at EXPO 1970 in Osaka was just such an example. The membrane covered an oval 142 m long and 83 m wide, and the shallow curve was made possible by support from a 32 rope net. At this world fair, which can be considered an experimental field for tent building, many technical and design possibilities that Frei Otto had been the first to point out were realised for the first time.

4 Exhibition pavilion at the 1964 World Fair in New York.

5 US pavilion at Expo 1970 in Osaka.

In 1970/71 Frei Otto's Warmbronn studio, Kenzo Tange and Ove Arup and Partners were planning the "City in Antarctica" project, an air hall spanning 2 km covering a residential town. This project became the forerunner for the "58° North" for Canada, in the region of the mineral oil sand of Alberta, which was intended for realization but never came to fruition.

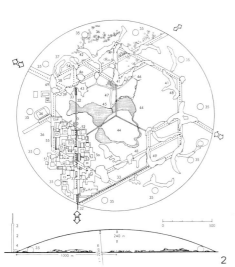

2

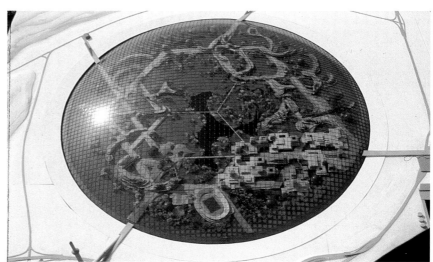

3

1

4

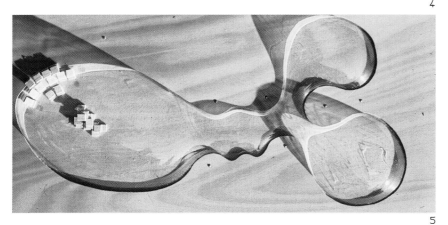

1–3 "City in Antarctica" project study, 1971, air hall as a protection against climate over a residential town.

4, 5 Design for a city in northern Canada, 58 degrees north, intended to be roofed with a light-permeable membrane. Models in plaster and perspex.

5

Water or other liquids can be used to support and tension membranes instead of air. Water containers and water towers, dams, mobile sewage treatment plants and flexible dikes are also possible with this structure and are already being manufactured. Membrane covers can also be supported by lower internal pressure. In this case the cover is evacuated. In principle this works according to the same rules that apply to constructions supported by higher internal pressure. Internal reinforcement, bracing, frames, supports and guys are shaping and structural elements. These constructions are used for greenhouses, for example, which are fixed to the ground by lower internal pressure to stop them from being blown away.

1

2

3

Suspended Constructions

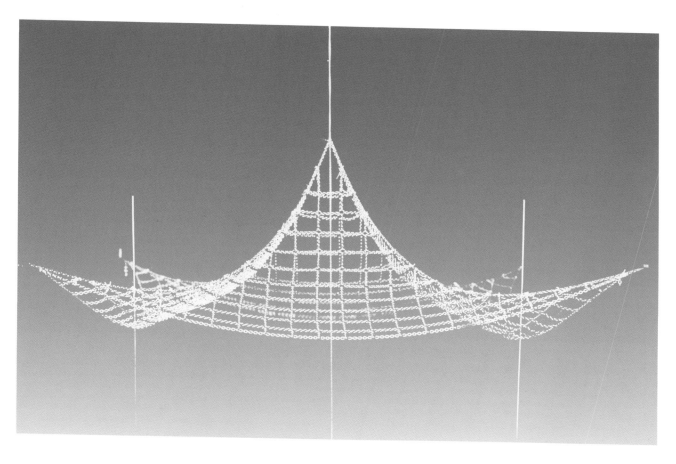

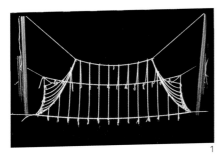

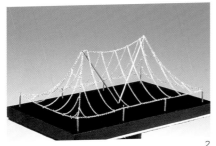

Unlike prestressed, three-dimensionally curved, plane, load-bearing constructions, suspended roofs are usually constructions that are curved on one side only, and stabilized without prestressing by their own weight. Their roof surface curves of its own accord in relation to the prevailing conditions. A suspended structure can be stabilized by sufficient self-weight, by stiffening the roof surface, or by guying.

The formal world of gravity suspended roofs, which are also known as heavy tents, is very varied. The pagoda and temple roofs of the Far East are made of freely suspended nets, originally made of bamboo lattices. Tension-loaded vegetable rods like wood and bamboo are used for the construction of suspended roofs as well as ropes made of vegetable fibres or steel. The form studies with models made of suspended chains produced by Frei Otto and his team revealed the formal world of historical suspended constructions, but they are also a key item in the design of suspended constructions made of nets, ropes and tension-loaded bars.

Several gravity suspended roofs span the rooms of the conference centre in Makkah, designed by Frei Otto with Rolf Gutbrod in 1965 and completed in 1972. Originally the competition design for a rope net structure was to be used for a conference centre in Riyadh, on the recommendation of King Faisal. This design was not realized, but led to the commissioning and building of the Makkah conference centre. The large complex on the edge of the city of Makkah consists of two areas (hotel, conference

1, 2 Suspension models to study the shape of Asian roofs.

rooms), which are arranged in such a way that each surrounds an inner courtyard. The suspended roofs are made up of supporting steel cables, a timber covering, thermal insulation and a corrugated aluminium roof skin.

The four conference rooms are connected by a corridor running round them. Ropes are stretched between the conference rooms, which together with radial ropes carry shady lath lattice elements. The shade in the inner courtyard of the adjacent mosque is supported by tubular steel stanchions.

Conference centre in Makkah:

3 View of the whole complex.

4 Interior of the large conference room.

5 The wooden sun protection lattices lie on a large-mesh latticework of steel cables.

6 The conference-centre mosque.

7. Roofs for shade in the inner courtyard of the mosque.

Frei Otto designed two suspended steel and glass constructions as a potentially quickly-built temporary accommodation for the medical academy in Ulm. Teaching and research work were to be accommodated in freely inserted lecture rooms and institutional rooms. Nine months were allowed from the start of design to completion of the building. The design was not realized, but formed the basis for a commission from the State Construction Office in Ulm for a building for the Fachhochschule in Ulm. On the same campus and very close to the university, a school was to be built that would use the experience of the IL's work in research and teaching. However, despite the most careful preparation in terms of engineering, including building physics and building technology, it was decided not to proceed further with the work.

1

2

3

1, 3 Glass and steel suspended structure over freely inserted rooms. Design for the medical academy in Ulm.

2, 4 Suspended structure for the Fachhochschule in Ulm.

5 Structure of the suspended roofs with glulam binders and supporting roof laths.

6 Model of the four pavilions.

7 View of the suspended roofs above the Wilkhahn extension building.

4

The extensions for Wilkhahn in Bad Münder show a new approach to the architectural design of premises for industrial production. The complex was built in 1987 and is designed in a sophisticated way appropriate to the different functions.

The four manufacturing departments are accommodated in four equal pavilions on a square ground plan with sides 22 m long. The suspended roofs over the pavilions consist of two three-hinged frames in each case as principle support, from which supporting roof laths are suspended. The three-hinged frames are arranged in the centre in such a way that a level roof surface is produced between these main bearers, and this was covered with glass. The interior is flooded with light and ensures a pleasant working atmosphere. The pavilions are arranged on a long building with a flat roof and form small, manageable units to which further buildings can be added if needed, without detracting from the overall architectural concept.

5

6

7

1

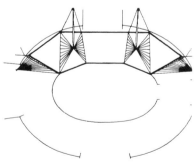

2

Frei Otto designed two different sized but similarly constructed gravity suspended roofs for the 1969/70 competition for roofing the stands of the Neckarstadion in Stuttgart (now Gottlieb-Daimler-Stadion) and the Olympic Stadium in Berlin.

The support system for the suspended roofs consists of steel cable suspended in parallel, steel rods laid on top and all supported by a crane-like jib system of compression bars and guy ropes. The outer segments of the stand roofs in each case are guyed to foundations with ropes.

A covering of transparent acrylic sheets was planned for both roofs. In order to establish the dynamic characteristics under wind and to work out the necessary weight of the structure for stability, the models were tested in aeroelastic wind tunnel experiments. Despite a high degree of effectiveness at low cost, neither of the designs was realized.

Competition design for stand roofing at the Berlin Olympic stadium, 1969:

1 Model.

2 Ground plan drawing.

Competition design for stand roofing for
the Gottlieb-Daimler-Stadion in Stuttgart:

3 Photo-collage.

4 Model.

6

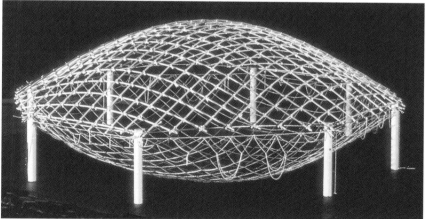

8

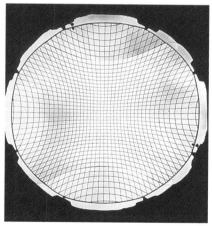

7

Many complex forms can be devised today purely mathematically using numerical methods, without experiments with models. But mastery of experimental model building methods was one of the most important requirements for the development of these mathematical programmes. It is scarcely possible to do without the model experiment today, and it continues to provide a basis for calculations.

8 Lattice shell model made of round wooden bars above the suspension form of the chain net, Salzburg Summer Academy.

139

The lattice shell in the design by architects Mutschler, Langner und Partner for the 1971 Federal Garden Exhibition in Mannheim was translated into architectonic form with the advice and co-operation of Frei Otto and his institute. The form-finding models and methods developed made it possible to establish the vault forms for the lattice shell, which consists of an even-mesh lattice of straight, continuous wooden slats. It was not only the design of this structure that was determined by self-forming processes, but the translation of the shape into architecture, the assembly of this lattice followed this principle as well: the rectangular lattice was first laid out on the level, then raised by scaffolding towers and given three-dimensional form. Here the connecting nodes on the slats remained pinned, so that the lattice could be moved like scissors and the form could be established. The lattice was fixed in

its form by tightening the lattice nodes, fixing the lattice at the edge and by additional reinforcement with a broad-mesh wire cable net and with the roof skin. The wooden laths are laid over each other crosswise in two or four laths with a mesh width (of the lattice that had just been laid out) of 50 cm. With a maximum span of 80 m and a roofed area of 7,400 sqm the lattice shell is one of the largest compression-loaded structures built.

Mannheim lattice shell, 1971:

1 Suspension model.

2 Exterior view.

3

5

6

4

3 The lattice was brought into its three-dimensional shape by the use of scaffolding towers.

4 Load experiments were carried out to establish the load-bearing capacity of the lattice shell: dustbins filled with water were hung at every 9th node, and the deformations could be measured by suspended plumb lines.

5 Evening photograph of the lattice shell without roof skin.

6 Covering the lattice shell with PVC-coated lattice fabric; this membrane has since been replaced.

7,8 Following page: interior views of the lattice shell.

7

8

The great KOCOMMAS (King's Office, Council of Ministers, Majilis al Shura) complex in Riyadh, Saudi Arabia, consists of several lattice shells, rope constructions and some solid multi-storey buildings.

The lattice shells cover reception and meeting rooms and inner courtyards. The lattices have a hexagonal mesh with equal-length bars in welded tubular steel and are covered with glass. Special aluminium umbrellas were developed as shade elements. The three-dimensional form of these bar constructions was arrived at in a suspended model, and the nodal points were also fixed in the suspended position.

The form of the branched supports was itself developed by self-forming processes. The great beauty of the structure rests on the harmonious combination of two constructions that emerged by self-formation. The project was designed down to the last detail, but could not be completed because of political developments.

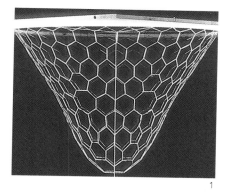

1 View of a hexagonal suspension model.

2 View into the model of the large hexagonal lattice shell, 70 m in diameter, supported by six branched columns. This dome was intended for the inner courtyard of the Council of Ministers, 1979.

1

2

Frei Otto's competition entry for the German pavilion at the 1992
Seville World Fair, a design for a lattice shell with several vaults,
won the 2nd prize. It proposed a metal lattice shell covered with
glass as a large cover for inserted terraces. Models were built in
different materials for the various phases of the form-finding
process: study models in plaster, wire fabric and wood to study
form and colour. Suspension models using chains helped to devise
the shape of the lattice shells. Design models in metal wire showed
the structure as a whole.

1 Model of the inserted terraces.

2 Design model for the competition for
the German pavilion in Seville, 1992.

The design for a lattice shell to cover the ruined Nikolaikirche in Hamburg was also produced in an all-embracing, complex form-finding process. The Nikolaikirche was destroyed by night bombing in the Second World War, and only the 147 m high tower survived. Frei Otto's studio had been commissioned by the city of Hamburg to prepare a report on the possible extension of the church as a museum and memorial for the night when it was bombed. The proposed roof structure over the destroyed nave consists of several successive glazed lattice domes and a painted crossing dome. The shape was devised by the use of a suspension model, the painting was designed by Bettina Otto using models in wire fabric and transparent sketching paper.

Lattice shell over the ruined Nikolaikirche in Hamburg, design 1992:

4 The painting for the crossing dome was designed by Bettina Otto and executed in the model.

5 Suspension model of the lattice shell.

6 Design model in wire fabric.

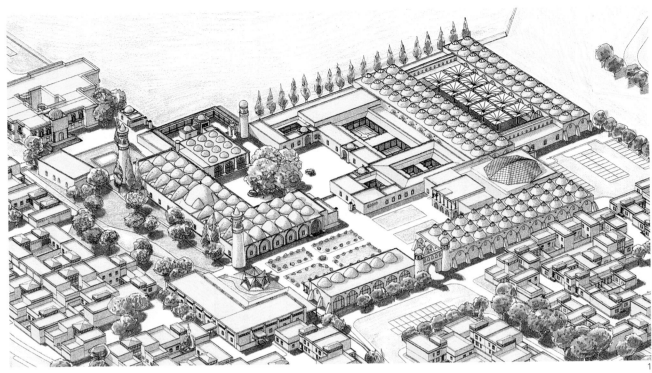

The scheme proposed by Bodo Rasch's office's in the competition to design a mosque extension and education center at the tomb of Imam Bukhari in Samarkand, included various large spaces roofed with domes. The form of these domes was determined by borrowing from traditional Islamic vaulted architecture, taking into consideration the need for stability in the face of the earthquakes that are a frequent occurrence. Brick has been a preferred building material in Samarkand from time immemorial, for bricks are simple to prepare, cheap and durable. Form is of particular importance for the stability of brick buildings, which are especially susceptible to earthquakes. This is also clear if one considers surviving historical buildings. The conical minarets of Central Asia for example have proved to be particularly stable.

Frei Otto developed an experimental method at the Institute for Lightweight Structure for investigating the stability of buildings in brick and natural stone. This makes it possible to investigate building forms with high stability against failure caused by their own weight, tilting, earthquakes and wind: models of brick and stone constructions built of small blocks are placed loose and unmortared on a tilting turntable. This establishes the inclination (measured in degrees or percentages) they collapse. A powerful earthquake (8–9 on the Richter scale) corresponds to an

1 Competition design for the Samarkand mosque extension.

2 The minaret of the Ulug Beg complex, destroyed by an earthquake, in Samarkand was supported by a structure designed by the Russian engineer Sûchov.

146

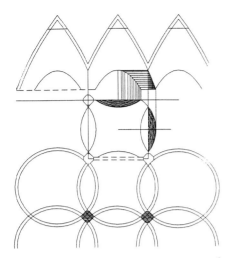

inclination of 30% and a horizontal acceleration of 0.2–0.3g. If a model remains standing safely at an inclination of 30%, then it is possible to assume that a building enlarged on the correct scale will not fail under horizontal forces of 0.3g.

Thus this experiment can be used to test a structure's behaviour when affected by horizontal forces. The results can be transferred to a building enlarged on the correct scale and thus the experiment is a key aid to judging the stability of masonry constructions when exposed to horizontal forces caused by earthquakes, wind etc. The stability of buildings made of preformed and mortared blocks is somewhat higher than that measured in the models.

1

2

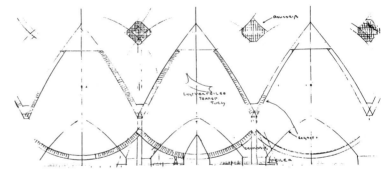

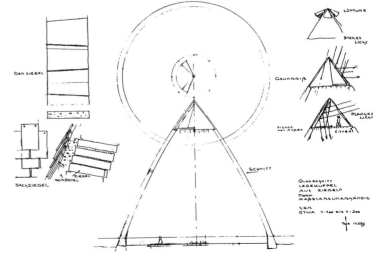

Competition design for the extension of the "Imam Bukhari" mosque in Samarkand:

Page **147**, ill. **3** This series of experiments with the tilting turntable shows the behaviour of the dome with skylight under horizontal load.

1 Computer drawing: ground plan and section of linked domes.

2 Model of the optimized dome form with skylight.

3 Frei Otto's sketches show the ground plan of linked domes and the optimized form in section.

3

Several experiments with a tilting turntable and a swinging bench were conducted in Atelier Warmbronn to find the form for the domes in Bodo Rasch's design. This led to a form that is particularly stable. The experimental results were integrated into the design and this led to domed constructions that do justice to the Islamic architectural tradition and to local conditions. The competition design won the 1st prize. This series of project related experiments was followed by numerous investigations of the stability of towers, arches, beams etc.

4 Section through the mosque.

5 This computer drawing shows the optimized dome forms on the ground plan of the mosque extension.

6 The dome forms provided by the experiment were modified for the final design.

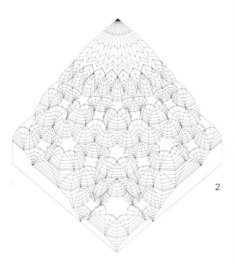

A vault shape that was developed not just from a structural point of view but also as a decorative element is the structure of the Muqarnas, which is made up of partial vaults. Muqarnas are found in all Islamic architecture, but their origins, load-bearing capacity and building techniques have hardly been researched or documented. Muqarnas are usually found as a transition from straight walls to a dome or half-dome (corbel vault) or also as a purely three-dimensional ornament in the form of suspended timber or stucco roofs.

The elements can be the size of a hand and carved in cedar, as in Morocco, or almost as high as a storey in masonry or plaster, as in Persia. Because of their similarity with natural forms they were also called stalactite domes in literature or compared with honeycombs.

In the first preliminary designs for the "Sliding Domes" project (see pp. 210–215), which involved vaulting a square space, several designs for Muqarnas were developed in Bodo Rasch's office. however this soon revealed that neither the analysis nor the design of Muqarnas could be handled with an architect's usual

1 Muqarnas above the entrance to the Sheikh Lutfallah mosque in Isfahan.

2 Isometric presentation of the Muqarna structure, designed for the Sliding Domes in Madinah.

3-7 Muqarnas, preliminary designs for the Sliding Domes.

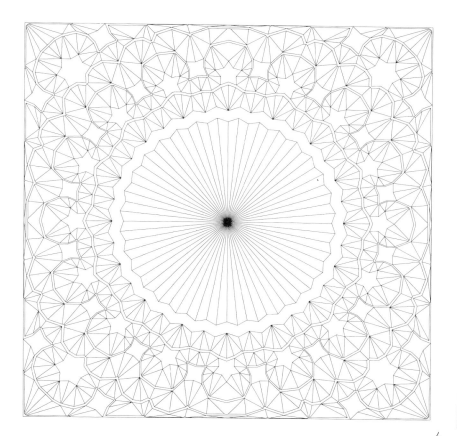

5

6

7

resources. These constructions are subject to mathematical laws that require a different approach.

A computer program was developed to analyse the geometry that can also be used to design these structure in combination with current CAD software. The program makes it possible to develop a curved surface into a plane, so that plans can be made for model building and realization. A three-axis milling machine can be programmed by translating the three-dimensional data into contour lines. Data can be transferred for further processing direct from the surface model to the control of a five-axis milling machine and recently to stereo-lithography as well. In this way models, moulds or also building parts for the Muqarnas can move straight from design to manufacture.

3 Design drawing, water-colour technique.

4 Ground plan, computer drawing.

5 Model of a mobile dome with Muqarnas.

6 The model was milled by a computer-controlled tool on the scale 1:20.

7 Three-dimensional computer simulation.

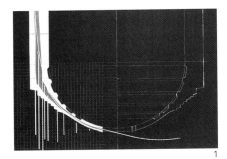

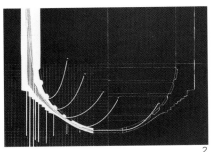

Frei Otto, working with colleagues and students, investigated the load-bearing capacity of the Pantheon in Rome as part of the IL's architectural history programme. Specially developed two- and three-dimensional suspension models provided information about the distribution, size and course of the pressure forces. Here the catenary was used not to establish an optimum vault form but to investigate the forces (and their course) that make the built dome form possible. Experiments using different suspended chain models showed among other things that, contrary to previous assumptions, ring compression forces as well as meridian forces were at work. The results (the structure of the model and the results of the experiments can be seen in study 11/84 at the Institute for Lightweight Structures) again show the value of experiments and model building methods not just for the analysis and interpretation of historical buildings but also for the design and planning of new constructions.

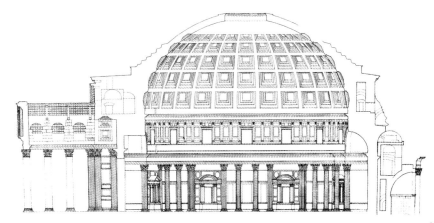

1, 2 Two-dimensional suspension chain model of the Pantheon dome:

1 Course of the pressure line under meridian direction pressure forces.

2 Investigation of the ring compression forces.

3 Pantheon, section after De Fine Licht.

4, 5 Three-dimensional suspension model. This form of the dome is produced if no ring compression forces are effective.

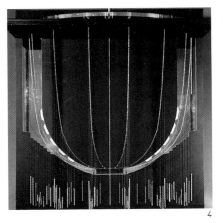

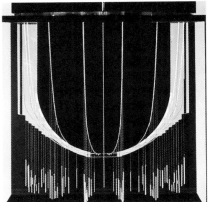

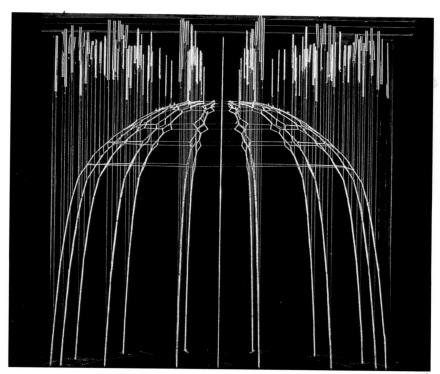

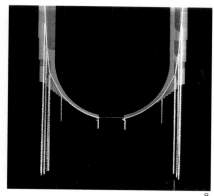

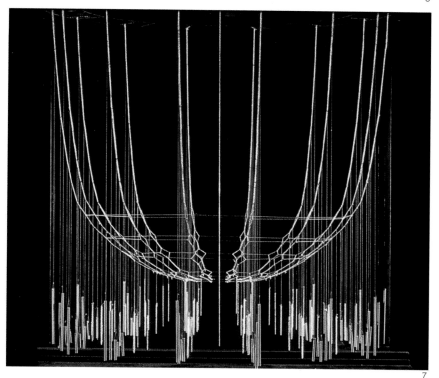

6 Three-dimensional suspension model of the dome with ring compression forces, photograph turned through 180°

7 Suspension model.

8 Two-dimensional suspension model.

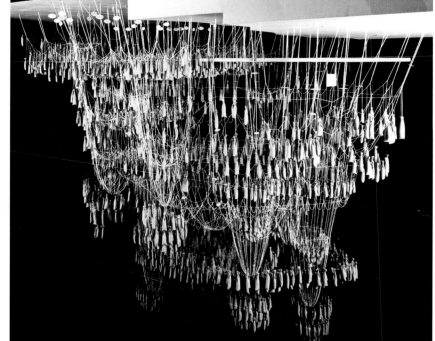

1 Gaudí's painting on a photograph of the suspension model for the "Colonia Güell" workers' estate shows his design.

2 Antoni Gaudí worked on the suspension model for over 10 years.

3 Original photograph (below) and reflection of the reconstruction model.

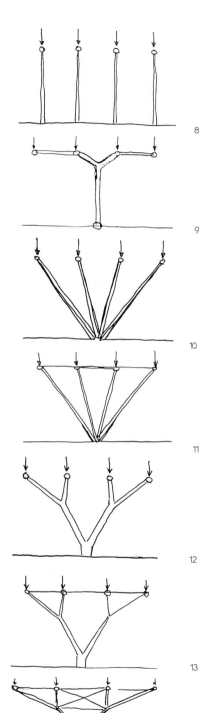

8

9

10

11

12

13

14

When looking for a form for compression loaded ceiling and roof plates knowledge of the minimum path system that can be investigated using soap films between plane-parallel glass plates is advantageous (sketch 15).

The direct path system is formed if rubber bands are stretched between points of application of force in the form of nails (sketch 16).

The path system with minimum detours is produced if thin threads are hung loosely between the points (sketch 17) and then moistened with water (sketch 18).

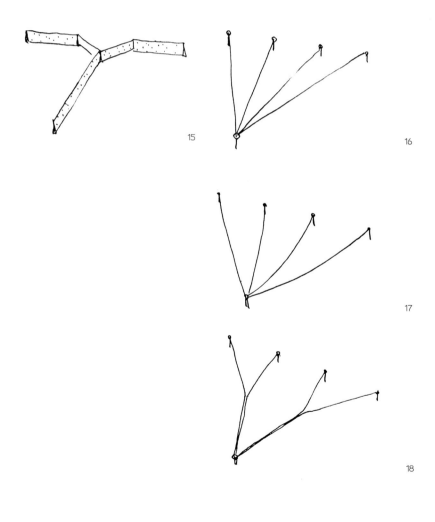

15

16

17

18

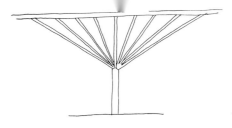

19

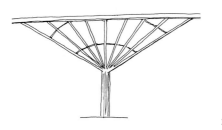

20

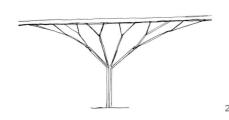

21

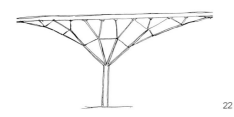

22

The fan structure (sketch 19), as used in timber and steel building, can be addressed as a materialized direct path network.

The "braced fan construction" (sketch 20) is more effective in many cases as the buckling lengths of the compression members are reduced.

The tree-like branched structure (sketch 21) is a materialized path network with minimum detours. It needs a relatively small amount of material and its load-bearing capacity can be increased by thin braces (sketch 22).

Plant support structures are also branched constructions. They can be compared with engineering branched constructions.

Both materialized direct path systems (e.g. umbels) and materialized path systems with minimum detours (e.g. in bushes and shrubs) occur. We find a combination with plane load-bearing constructions in the branched ribs and the surface of grass, tree and herb leaves.

The difference from current building constructions lies in function. In plants both the forces applied to the many short-lived solar collectors (leaves) and the liquids needed for survival have to be transported.

The photographs show studies and projects on the subject of branching from Frei Otto's work, who has been working on the theory of optimizing frame constructions intensively since 1974.

1 Suspension model using stiffened threads stiffened with Polyester and inverted. Preliminary design for an exhibition hall, 1960.

2 Branched constructions.

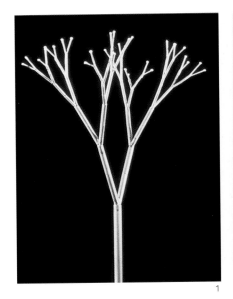

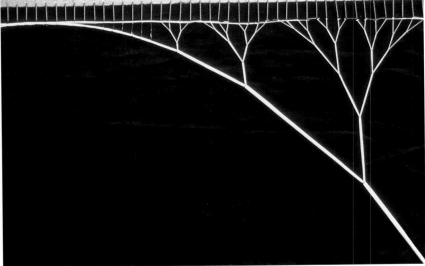

1 Model of a branched support structure.

2 Study model using threads to establish minimalized detours, 1983.

3 Aluminium cast of a pneumatically tensioned branch structure. Frei Otto's sculpture hangs in the small inner courtyard of the Museum for Architecture in Frankfurt.

4 Branched constructions as support constructions for a hexagonal lattice shell in the KOCOMMAS project. Model in tubular aluminium.

5 Drawing by Frei Otto, 1980.

6 This model made of steel springs was built in Atelier Warmbronn in 1983 to study bracing forces in tension-loaded constructions.

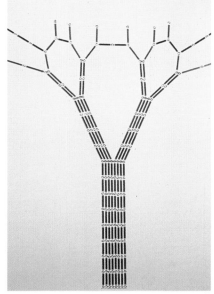

In 1991 the Federal Ministry of Research and Technology commissioned Frei Otto's studio to prepare a report from both an ecological and an aesthetic point of view on the design of a new kind of track for the German magnet railway system, in co-operation with Sir Edmund Happold of Bath. There is hardly a more difficult but also more fascinating task for architects and engineers than developing tracks that are aesthetic, ecological and economic, all at the same time. The run of the line and the design of the track play a key role for the magnet express train. The track swallows over three quarters of the cost of the transport system. It carries the linear magnets that propel the vehicle and make it hover.

The magnet express train is a very rapid means of transport. It is considered environmental friendly and sensible in terms of energy. It relieves road traffic and also short-haul air traffic.

Development of the vehicle is well advanced. It has been tested and is ready to go into service. It travels at 300–400 km/h, with a top speed of about 500 km/h. The structural form and aesthetic acceptability of track play an important part in the feasibility of the whole magnet train project.

The vehicle needs new tracks that will not place an additional burden on fields, woods, villages and towns. Even though the trains "hover" they place considerable loads on the track. This has to be extremely precisely built, and resistant to deformation. high-level lines that take the vehicles through the air and only touch the ground at a few points are desirable.

The existing track for the test line in the Emsland was intended for development of the vehicles. It is now necessary to develop the track of the future.

The new track must not be a blight on its surroundings. It should

Designs for the magnet train track:

1, 2   Structural form with fan-like branches.

3 The filigree latticework beam represents a static-dynamic continuum.

4 The various structural forms show the working path from solid beam to filigree latticework beam.

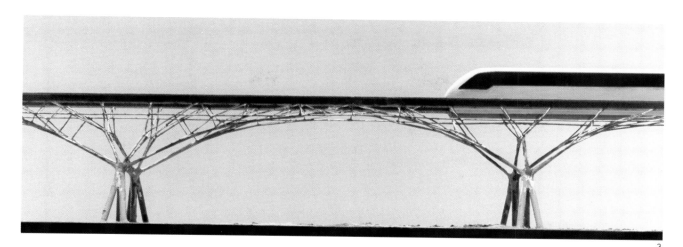

3

fit in visually with the landscape in such a way that it forms an inconspicuous part of the ecological system through which it is travelling. To this end it is necessary that it takes up very little air space and ground surface, that it is extremely light (e.g. by omitting any inessential construction material), and that it exerts as little force as possible on its foundations. It should be easy to assemble and should not disturb the environment either when it is being built or when the route is changed or if it becomes necessary to dismantle it (ground water stocks, the plant and animal kingdoms, existing paths, roads, water courses, railways).

The working party examined ten different structural forms, calculated and optimized about sixty variants statically and showed a way in which further intensive research, planning and practical tests could find a track that is aesthetic and ecological and considers the prevailing economic conditions.

In working on form-finding the physical methods for determining the direct path system, minimum paths and minimalized detours were applied.

The models exhibited show the working path from the solid concrete or steel beam to the filigree lattice beam in corrosion-proof steel, intended to be constructed as a static-dynamic continuum.

The search for a form for the magnet express track also shows prospects for new tracks for high-speed trains in the traditional railway system.

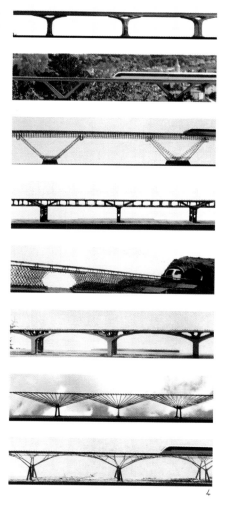

4

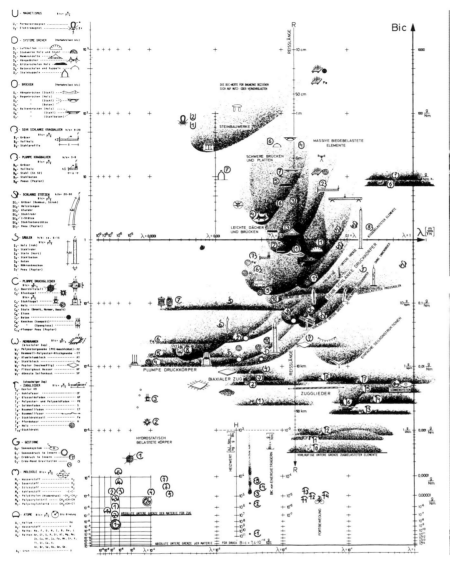

6

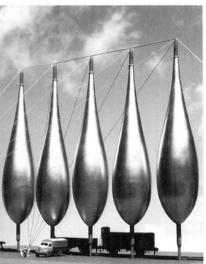

7

Der Bic ist definiert als das Verhältnis von aufgewendeter Masse (m) zum Tra (F·s). Das Produkt aus der zu übertragenden Kraft (F) und der zugehörigen Obertragungsstrecke (s) wird als Tra bezeichnet.

$$Bic = \frac{m}{Tra} \left[\frac{g}{Nm}\right] = \frac{m}{\sum\limits_{i=1}^{n} F_i \cdot s_i}$$

Für die relative konstruktive Schlankheit gilt: $\lambda = \frac{s}{\sqrt{F}} \left[\frac{m}{\sqrt{N}}\right]$

F= Kraft in Newton [N], s= Obertragungsstrecke in m, m= Masse des betrachteten Objekts in g.

Die R-Achse beschreibt die Reisslänge, gemessen in km; 1 dtex = 1g je 10km:

$$R = \frac{100}{Bic} = \frac{cN}{dtex}$$

5

1 Pneumatically supported tower structure.

2, 3 Model studies for the minimal surface cooling tower (see chapter on net constructions).

4 Cross-section forms for tall cooling towers.

5 Bic-l diagram, 1985 version.

6 Project for a water tower, model study.

7 Suspended flexible containers for liquids and bulk materials.

171

Problem waste represents an ever-increasing burden for air and ground water; it is probably an unavoidable evil of modern society. Frei Otto suggested and required years ago that rubbish should be disposed of under large protective coverings. With Bodo Rasch and Sir Edmund Happold, he developed a new disposal system that offers secure protection against noise, dust and ground water, and also makes it possible to clean the air given off. The core of this system is a large movable cover made of a rope net with 12 mm thick non-corroding cables and a mesh of 50 mm. This net is sealed with a recyclable plastic sheet about 1.0 mm thick, partially transparent and partially light-permeable and light-reflecting, whose edges are fastened to the ground not with expensive concrete anchors but simply weighted with earth ramparts in a very simple way. The interior is lit by daylight, no energy is wasted on artificial light.

The roof, which can span up to 500 m freely and be up to 50 m high, is dome-like, and characterized by the veil of the net; it is also the best solution in landscape terms. A slight excess pressure in the interior of only 0.003 bars presses the membrane against the rope net and stabilizes the cover as a whole.

This structure for the cover is extremely flexible in principle. Even large deformation caused by ground settling or changes to the edges do not present any problems. The hall changes form, ground surface and volume even while it is in use. It moves continually as required by disposal needs, without needing breaks for demolition and rebuilding.

The earth ramparts are resited by mechanical diggers and a strip of net and membrane is removed at one side of the cover and added on at the other. Thus the cover moves slowly over the sealed heap of refuse and offers space for new problem waste. When the heap of waste has reached a certain height its surface is sealed with a permanent sealing strip, then it is planted and transformed into a well-designed landscape park.

With a small initial quantity of refuse the cover is small as well, and this means small initial investment. Low material costs, reasonable starting and overall costs are the features of this new eco-technical system. It can be installed by the dump operators themselves, without the need for specialist firms, though constant scientific checks are needed.

1-4 The illustrations show the design in model and drawing for the moving cover for dumps for the disposal of harmful waste.

DIE WANDERNDE HÜLLE

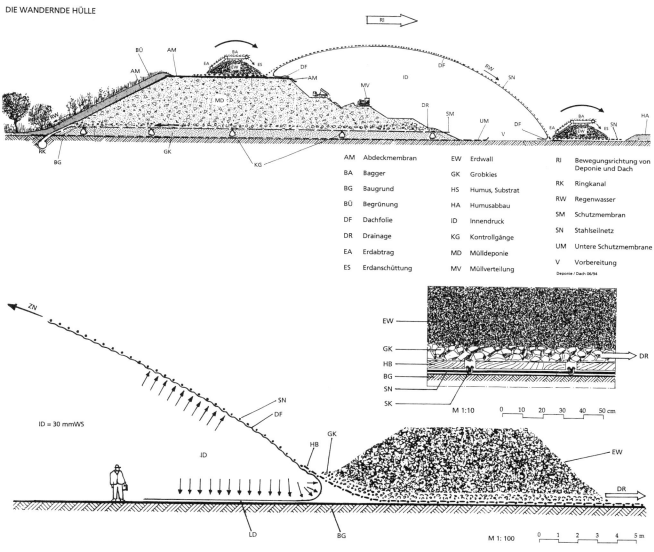

AM	Abdeckmembran	EW	Erdwall	RI	Bewegungsrichtung von Deponie und Dach
BA	Bagger	GK	Grobkies		
BG	Baugrund	HS	Humus, Substrat	RK	Ringkanal
BÜ	Begrünung	HA	Humusabbau	RW	Regenwasser
DF	Dachfolie	ID	Innendruck	SM	Schutzmembran
DR	Drainage	KG	Kontrollgänge	SN	Stahlseilnetz
EA	Erdabtrag	MD	Mülldeponie	UM	Untere Schutzmembrane
ES	Erdanschüttung	MV	Müllverteilung	V	Vorbereitung

Deponie / Dach 06/94

M 1:10

0 10 20 30 40 50 cm

ID = 30 mmWS

M 1: 100

0 1 2 3 4 5 m

4

1 This apparatus shows the position of the sun and the shadows it casts for any point on the earth at any time.

2 Shades for the octagonal lattice shell for the planned KOCOMMAS project in Riyadh, Saudi Arabia (see p. 141).

3, 4 Shade in the desert, 1972.

5 Sketches for solar energy plants.

6

7

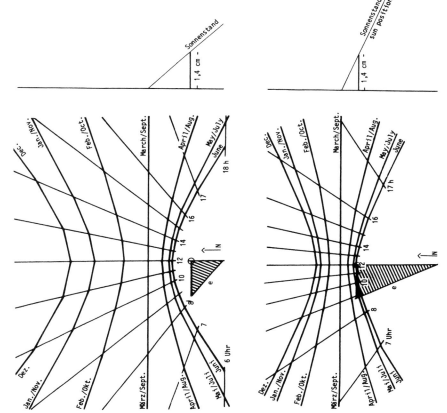

Stuttgart   48,8° Nord
Stuttgart   48,8° North

IL 30 (1984)

Nördlicher Wendekreis   23,5°
Northern tropic   23,5°

8

6,7 Prototypes of the 5 m x 5 m solar-powered umbrellas in Saudi Arabia, 1987 (see pp. 188-189).

8 Horizontal sundials.

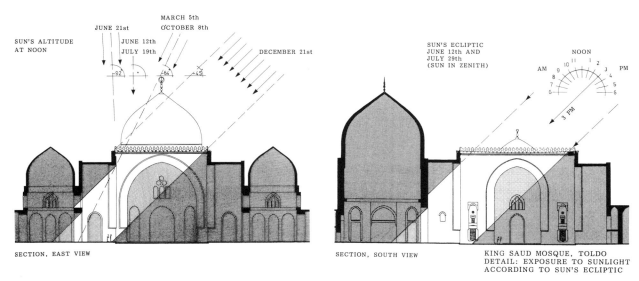

SUN'S ALTITUDE
AT NOON

JUNE 21st   MARCH 5th
          JUNE 12th   OCTOBER 8th
          JULY 19th

-92   -64   -45

DECEMBER 21st

SUN'S ECLIPTIC
JUNE 12th AND
JULY 29th
(SUN IN ZENITH)

NOON

AM   10 11   1   2   PM
     8   3
    7   4
    6   5
                  6

3 PM

SECTION, EAST VIEW

SECTION, SOUTH VIEW

KING SAUD MOSQUE, TOLDO
DETAIL: EXPOSURE TO SUNLIGHT
ACCORDING TO SUN'S ECLIPTIC   1

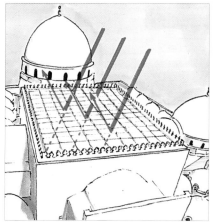

In southern countries considerable problems are caused by strong sunlight. Internal courtyards with low air circulation in particular heat up very quickly so that in the summer months temperatures of over 50° in the shade are no rarity.

Bodo Rasch's office has developed and built a number of convertible roofs for the internal courtyards of mosques, and they have made a significant contribution to improving the climate of the building.

The inner courtyards of the mosque in Madinah are roofed with a total of 39 convertible shades, 12 folding umbrellas and 27 mobile domes (see pp. 193-197, 208-215). The first measurements confirm that the convertible roofs have a strong influence on the climate of the building: extreme values were reduced by over 10%.

But in order to be able to make quantitative predictions about climatic improvement using convertible roofs, a simulation model was developed in Bodo Rasch's office. The calculation model, which can simulate complex systems with free convection, phase changes and infra-red emissions, is based on the finite element methods, which permits precise statements about dynamic systems. Fundamental physical values were used for the physical description of the complex system, rather than just formulae: values for conductivity, heat capacity, spectral heat reflection and spectral emissive power were used to calculate heat transmission in the masonry.

32 sensors were installed in various places in the Prophet's holy Mosque in Madinah; they measure and store data on temperature, relative humidity, wind speed, solar irradiation, heat radiation and air pressure. This data collection ended in December 1994, and the results of the evaluation are due in summer 1995.

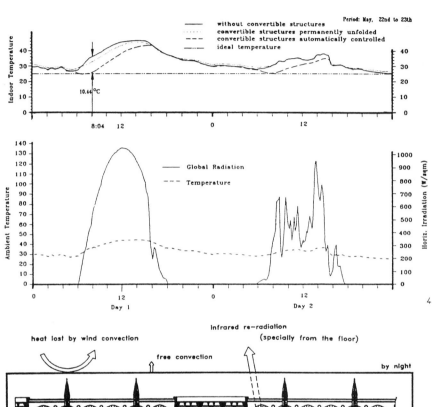

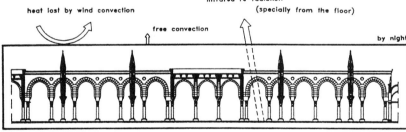

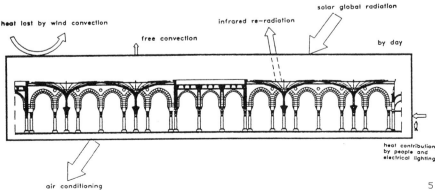

Studies for climate regulation with convertible roofs.

1 Study as part of a design for a toldo as a shade in the inner courtyard of the King Saud Mosque in Jeddah, Saudi Arabia.

2,3 These drawings illustrate the principle of climatic regulation by closing the shade during the day and opening it at night (see p. 183).

4,5 Study for climate regulation of the inner courtyards of the Prophet's holy Mosque in Madinah using large convertible shades (see pp. 191-194).

6 View of the convertible screens in one of the two large inner courtyards of the Prophet's holy Mosque in Madinah, 1993.

Convertible Constructions

The idea of building variably and thus allowing adaptation to changing weather conditions is very old indeed. Even in ancient times mobile roofs were used as a protection against the sun and to regulate the climate in rooms. Coverings were placed over small courtyards with an area of no more than a few square metres, right up to the Roman custom of roofing large theatres and amphitheatres with the so-called vela. Perhaps the best-known example of traditional convertible roofs to provide shade are the toldos (Spanish: awning) that are still used in Spain today (2). Cotton awnings are stretched between parallel wires throughout streets in whole suburbs. They can be moved from the houses, roofs or street with simple rope mechanisms. These simple awnings show that solid and light construction complement each other very well.

Convertible roofs are constructed in such a way that their form can be altered as often as wished and in a relatively short time. They solve problems that cannot be tackled by other methods. The diversity of constructions used ranges from simple awnings to relatively complex mobile domes, of the kind that have long been used in Morocco and were put up by Bodo Rasch in 1992 to provide shade for the 27 inner courtyards of the Prophet's holy Mosque in Madinah.

Frei Otto's development of new light constructions that can be used to span wide areas with the smallest possible outlay in terms of materials and mass, has attracted a great deal of attention to the variability of light constructions. His ground-breaking work did not just produce a new generation of convertible roofs, but new, highly efficient movement systems and particularly suitable materials were also developed.

These developments make it possible to realize buildings that are there only when they are needed: automatically controlled large-scale tents that can be in place in a few minutes in order to provide protection against the weather.

The roof over the 'Masque de Fer' open-air theatre was built in 1965 as a first convertible roof with external oblique mast and centrally gathered roof-skin. The frame structure of the mast is optimized by the small number of compression-loaded elements, and additionally multiple guying means reduced buckling lengths. The 1000 sqm roof skin can be in place in a very few minutes and covers an area of 800 sqm. It is suspended by trolleys at 16 points, and each trolley has its own traction cable and winch.

1,2 Fold formation in para rubber fabric suspended from three points.

3 Traditional toldos providing shade in the streets of Cordoba, Spain.

4 Toldos in the inner courtyard of the Uthman Katkhuda mosque, Cairo.

5 Convertible structure over the casino of the open-air theatre in Cannes.

3

4

5

2

The open-air productions in the ruined Stiftskirche in Bad hersfeld required a convertible roof structure that did not affect the historic building and did not impair the spatial impression given by the Romanesque setting (1 and 2).

Frei Otto's Berlin studio's 1959 competition entry eight years later led to a commission to provide a design that could be realized. The convertible roof in Bad hersfeld was built in 1968. The structure consists of a gatherable membrane roof supported by a central mast. The mast stands by the nave of the ruin, and it is guyed by two cables at the rear and 14 guy ropes running like rays over the nave at the front. The guys over the nave are at the same time ferry ropes for the self-driving cable tractors from which the roof skin is suspended. The cable tractors were developed specially for this roof by haushahn of Stuttgart; they are still in service, giving undiminished performance after 25 years.

The roof can be in place within four minutes, and covers an area of 1315 sqm. The form of the roof was devised using a mobile function model at a scale of 1:50, the fundamental problems of the gathering and folding of the roof skin were examined and questions relating to the fitting process clarified. The membrane, originally grey in colour, was still almost as strong as ever in 1993, but it was replaced by a membrane that was white but impermeable to light.

1

Bodo Rasch's office was presented with a similar project in 1988 (3-5). A convertible membrane structure had to be fitted into the historical castle for the open-air theatre in Wiltz in Luxemburg in such a way that neither the impressive appearance of the place nor the character of the open-air plays was impaired or changed.

The support structure of the roof runs round the spectator and stage areas. It consists of tubular steel supports, guy ropes and a ring rope. The folded membrane is parked under a light protective roof opposite the stage, and thus does not interfere with the spectators' view. In bad weather the roof is moved into place with an electronically controlled roof traction mechanism and automatically pretensioned in its final position.

The extended, pretensioned roof (with an area of about 1200 sqm) forms a generous saddle area that protects stage and auditorium to an equal extent. The edge of the roof curves up towards the stage to give a view of the historical castle setting. The broad roof area is structured with round anchor plates above which the membrane is suspended from the support cables in such a way that it can move. The whole roof structure can be removed at the end of the theatre season and then rebuilt without difficulty. Rope tractors could have been used similar to those that have proved very successful as a drive mechanism in Bad Hersfeld, but the firm who built the roof used a different mechanism that is technically and aesthetically less attractive.

3

4

5

1 It takes less than 4 minutes to extend the membrane roof over the ruined Stiftskirche in Bad Hersfeld.

2 View of the roof from above.

3-5 Convertible roof for the open-air theatre in Wiltz, Luxemburg, 1988:

3 Model presentation.

4 The extended membrane roof forms a large, coherent saddle area.

5 Folded membrane behind the spectators.

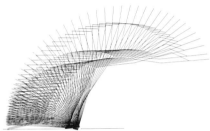

1

1 Extension curve and model of the "Cabrio" folding stand cover, of which one prototype was built, 1986.

2 Convertible roof for a multi-media stadium.

2

The great advantages of convertible roofs to provide shade lies in the fact that the climate of a building can be regulated in a way that is very effective ecologically and economically. The cooling effect is achieved by preventing the direct sunlight from reaching the surfaces of the building covered by the roof. Stored warmth can be released by opening the roof. This means that more energy is re-radiated than shines in during the day. The energy dynamics brought into being between all the surfaces involved means that in a few days the shaded surfaces are significantly cooler than their surroundings.

In 1987 Bodo Rasch devised a toldo to provide shade for the courtyard of the Quba Mosque in Madinah, Saudi Arabia. The two parts of the structure are suspended on cables and are moved into position laterally and folded. Support is provided by two lattice tube bearers on the long sides.

The translucent membrane is made up of two layers, a lower and an upper net held together in strips by aluminium tubes. They are suspended on rope trolleys by support cables and are moved by electric motors.

During the summer months the temperature in the building as a whole is lowered to a pleasantly moderate level. In winter the principle is reversed: heat is stored inside the mosque by opening the roof during the day and closing it at night.

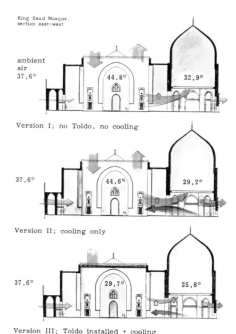

King Saud Mosque, section east-west

ambient air 37,6° 44,8° 32,9°

Version I; no Toldo, no cooling

37,6° 44,6° 29,2°

Version II; cooling only

37,6° 29,7° 25,8°

Version III; Toldo installed + cooling

3

4

5

3 The climate in the inner courtyard of the King Saud Mosque in Jeddah was examined in a climate regulation study with the aid of convertible roof shading.

4,5 Toldo for the inner courtyard of the Quba Mosque, Madinah, Saudi Arabia, 1987.

Umbrellas

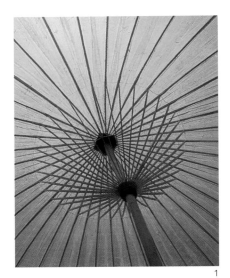

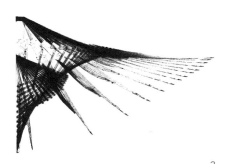

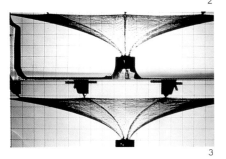

It can be presumed that the umbrella is the oldest type of convertible and very useful roof construction with a small span. It is an archetype, related in form and structure to the yurt and the tepee. Umbrellas are known to all cultures as a sign of majesty, a symbol of spiritual or secular power. The umbrella is rather like a mobile baldacchino, and symbolizes the significance and position of the person protected. It was always a sign of special presence, both for early Chinese emperors and Egyptian pharaohs.

The traditional umbrella appeared in various forms, according to material, shape and symbolic content. The simplest form consists of a central rod to which rigid or mobile bars are attached. These umbrellas were covered with fabric, leaves, leather, paper, feathers etc. The tension loaded membranes, the roof ribs, the bars and the central rod make up a constructional unit.

In the 50s Frei Otto developed a new umbrella form based on the minimum surface principle. The exclusively tension loaded membrane of the funnel-shaped umbrella is now stretched under the compression-loaded bars. This construction type made it technically and structurally possible to build very large, convertible umbrellas.

The first umbrellas of this kind, built by Frei Otto for the 1955 Federal Garden Exhibition in Kassel were fixed; he constructed the first convertible large umbrella for the Cologne Federal Garden Exhibition in 1971 (19 m diameter/project director Bodo Rasch). The interesting feature of this umbrella is the shape of the rib system. The length of the umbrella arms was reduced telescopically when it was folded, and the movement of the arms was controlled by a curved track in such a way that the umbrellas could be operated individually in any sequence wished, even though they overlap. The membrane of the Cologne umbrella is made up of PVC-coated polyester fabric. The umbrellas are still in use today, but they are opened and closed very infrequently; the process takes about 2.5 minutes.

For British pop group Pink Floyd's American tour in 1978 Frei Otto built a group of ten convertible umbrellas (each 4.5 m in diameter); they could be brought up from under the stage when needed and then opened up.

The great beauty of these very simply constructed umbrellas inspired many subsequent projects, including the umbrellas designed by Bodo Rasch and his team to provide shade for the great mosques in Saudi Arabia.

1 Traditional Japanese bamboo umbrella, covered with paper.

2 Movement sequence for the tips of the arms at the Federal Garden Exhibition in Cologne, 1971.

3 Soap film model of the Pink Floyd umbrella.

4 Umbrellas at the Cologne Federal Garden Exhibition, 1971.

5 Opening or closing takes 2.5 minutes.

6,7 Pink Floyd umbrella, 1978.

A convertible shade was to be developed for the great mosque in Makkah; it had to be very light so that it did not place too great a load on the structure of the building. The suggestion was made that solar powered square umbrellas should be used. They were developed especially for the purpose and at 240 kg were relatively light. The membrane sides are 5 m long, which corresponds with the building's support grid. The funnel shape of the double-curved membrane, which establishes the shape of the individual umbrellas, was derived from soap film studies. The umbrellas were provided with a wind-monitoring device that caused them to close at wind speeds over 12m/sec. They are thus never exposed to high wind speeds and so could be scaled for smaller forces and very light in structure. Integrated photovoltaic solar power generation means that they can be opened and closed independently. After a development period of only six months, two small series of 12 umbrellas each were built and tested on the Arabian coast under extreme climatic conditions.

1

1 This function model at a scale of 1:5 was used to check the frame geometry.

2 Prototypes on the Red Sea coast, 1987.

2

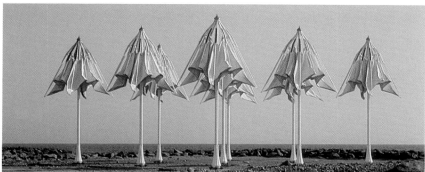

4

3

3 Prototypes on the coast; opening. When open the umbrellas are 5.4 m high, when closed 6.5 m.

4 This view from below shows the solar cells built into the umbrella arms.

3

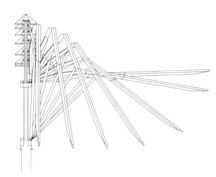

1

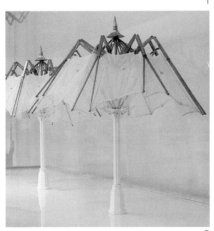

2

An umbrella with sides 10 m long was developed as a convertible roofing for the large external areas around the Prophet's holy Mosque in Madinah. The arms of the umbrellas are constructed in such a way that they fold while closing and the umbrella, which has an overall height of less than 9 m when closed, reaches a maximum span of over 12 m.

Another special feature of this umbrella are the forked arms, which enable doubling of the suspension points on the membrane. In this way, with 16 membrane suspensions, only eight arms have to be attached in the immediate vicinity of the mast. A prototype was built and tested.

The umbrella frame and mast are welded steel constructions, and a newly developed Teflon fabric was used as membrane for the first time.

Against the background of this technical knowledge Bodo Rasch was able to realize another umbrella project in 1992, bringing together all the insights acquired up to that time.

1 Folding curve for an arm of the 10 x 10 m umbrella.

2 Part of the mechanical model with 6 umbrellas on a scale 1:20.

3 The prototype was set up near Stuttgart in 1988 and has been tested since then.

4 The 17 x 18 m umbrellas in the inner courtyard of the Prophet's holy Mosque Madinah.

192

4

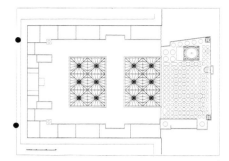

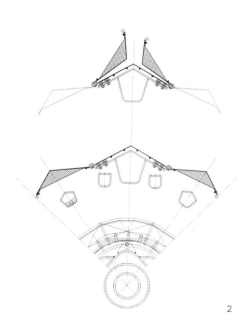

Twelve large umbrellas were built as a convertible roof for the two large courtyards of the Prophet's holy Mosque in Madinah. Their dimensions, an area of 17 m x 18 m and an eaves height of 14 m when open, were determined by the proportions of these courtyards. Six umbrellas per courtyard, with funnel-shaped membranes, form a translucent vault stretching between the columns and arcades that border the courtyard, joining with them to form a wide, light space.

Unlike the Cologne umbrellas, arranged irregularly in an open space, the courtyard umbrellas are subject to strict architectural rules. Particular attention was paid to the fact that the open courtyard can be transformed into a closed hall in less than two minutes by opening the umbrellas – an extremely dramatic procedure that requires a certain amount of choreography as well as making demands on technology and geometry.

Consistent and logical use of this convertible roof as appropriate to major changes in the external climate, fundamentally influences and improves the energy balance of the building.

The umbrella frame, mast, arms and supports are welded in close-grained steel; the shape of each supporting member is determined by the particular gradient of forces. The umbrella arms are mobile and placed at the upper end of a hydraulic cylinder that is central on the mast in such a way that its upward and downward movements are transmitted to the umbrella frame, thus opening or closing the umbrella. The hydraulic units that create the necessary oil pressure for the movement of the cylinders, and the electronic control that checks, regulates and synchronizes all the movement of the umbrellas are housed centrally in the basement of the building. A wind-monitoring device integrated into the electronic controls prevents the umbrellas being operated at wind speeds above 12 m/sec. When designing these umbrellas, which with a span of 24 m are so far the largest of their kind, a great deal of care was taken with the shapes of the umbrellas when folded and the folding of the membrane. Extremely light movable carbon fibre flaps are fixed along the diagonal arm sides and connected to the umbrella frame by an articulated lever mechanism, so that they are linked to its movements. As the umbrella is closed the flaps close to support the folding of the fabric. When closed they and the fixed sheet metal cladding in the upper arm area provide a solid cover for the membrane, which is thus completely packed up, a principle that was used for the first time for these umbrellas. The membrane consists of a specially developed PTFE (Teflon) fabric that has quite new qualities especially when being folded and for the first time really reveals

1 Roof aspect with the 12 open umbrellas completed in 1992.

2 Cross-section through a diagonal arm with open and closed carbon fibre composite flaps.

3

the fabric nature of this type of structure. This fabric is also UV resistant, chemically resistant, fireproof and shows minimum surface friction; it thus comes very close to the desired ideal for a membrane material for convertible constructions.

3 The umbrella while the membrane is being fitted.

1 When closed the six light carbon fibre flaps and the fixed sheet metal cladding in the upper arm area provide a solid cover for the membrane, which is thus completely packed up. This principle was used for the first time for these umbrellas.

2 Detail of the column with integrated lighting and outlet vents for the cold air from the air-conditioning system. These were specially designed to distribute the cold air silently about 11 m into the space. The system was constructed in co-operation with Dr. Kamal Ismail, the architect responsible for the mosque extension.

3 View of the six open umbrellas from above.

4 Inner courtyard with the open umbrellas. They provide cooling shade for the pilgrims.

3

4

To solve problems of space in the Muna valley, which is too narrow to accommodate all the pilgrims, Frei Otto and Bodo Rasch (with Sami Angawi) developed very flexible yet simple frame tents that can be pitched anywhere, even on steep mountain slopes. The tents can be adapted to the topography of the mountains enclosing the valley in such a way that the character of the steep mountain slopes is preserved. The support structure for these pilgrim tents, which are the usual 4 m x 4 m, is an aluminium frame, and the covering is in the traditional cotton sailcloth. Guys and pegging are not needed, and so the tents can be pitched on any type of ground. 20–30 tents would make sensible units to form small camps that are given a common infrastructure of water containers, washing facilities and access by steps. The constructions can be struck after the hajj without leaving damages or traces of their presence in the landscape. A few prototypes were built and tested with support from the hajj Research Centre in 1981.

1 View of a tented city during the hajj.

2–4 Prototypes of the frame tent developed by Frei Otto, Bodo Rasch and Sami Angawi were pitched on the mountain slopes near Muna in 1981.

Containers with toilets and ritual washing facilities were developed for sanitation purposes. It is not possible to build sluice sewerage systems because the tented cites are used for so short a time. For this reason electricity and water, and above all sewerage facilities, are provided by a mobile system independent of the supply networks. The sanitary units are conceived in such a way that they can be built in various sizes and levels of equipment and thus adapted to the particular conditions. A membrane with the proportions of the traditional pilgrim's tent is used to cover them, so that these units also blend harmoniously into the picture of the tented city. The containers are serviced in a central yard and taken from there to the individual sites by lorries.

The containers can be assembled ready for use within an hour: the side walls are opened up, the membrane roof is pitched, the

6

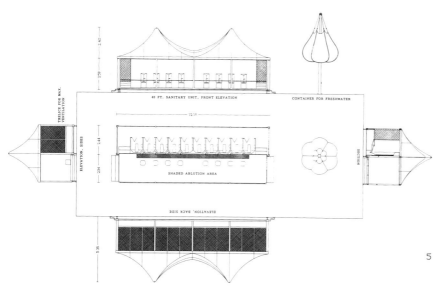
5

7

pipes put together and connected to the water containers. If the unit cannot be connected to an existing electricity supply power is provided by generators. The membrane structure for the fresh water containers is also a new development. Watertight PVC fabric is suspended from a mast and water pressure makes it adopt the shape determined by its cut.

5 Ground plan, sections and views of the sanitary containers.

6 The photo-collage shows the container with membrane roof in position in a tented city.

7 This receptacle for water was developed to provide fresh water for the containers.

The bottlenecks that occur in the stream of pilgrims on foot during the hajj were localized and analysed in a wide-ranging series of investigations. Mathematical models were used to calculate the capacity of the Mataf area in the courtyard of the Al haram mosque in Makkah: during the hajj each pilgrim has to go round the Ka'aba seven times ("Tawaf"), and many pilgrims try to touch the black stone (Al hajar Al Aswad) in the south-eastern corner of the Ka'aba while doing this. The entire Mataf area is often filled with a compact stream of humanity that makes any movement impossible. The simulation models that were developed made it possible to provide very precise statements on the effects of various structural approaches on the capacity of the Mataf area. Thus they provide important decision-making criteria guaranteeing a smooth flow of movement even at the preliminary planning stage.

Bodo Rasch's office developed a computer program normally used in particle physics for analysing the masses of pilgrims at that time. This program simulates the movement of each individual pedestrian and means that their complex movements can be recorded.

These pictures are part of a series of experiments to simulate a situation where two paths meet and lead to an object at which the pilgrims pause briefly and then move on.

1, 2 Major infrastructural problems are caused by the increasing number of pilgrims during the hajj.

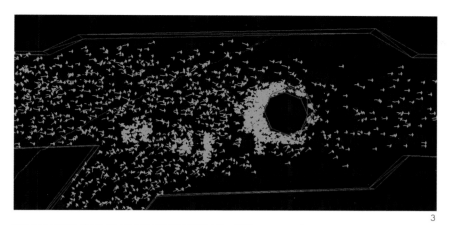

3

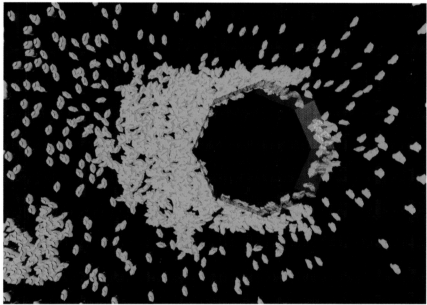

4

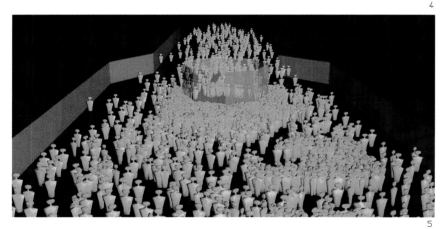

5

3-5 Computer simulation of pedestrian traffic, 1994.

1

2

1-5 Convertible umbrellas in the inner courtyard of the Prophet's Holy Mosque in Madinah, directly adjacent to the old building.
The lower part of the umbrellas was designed by Dr. Kamal Ismail, chief architect of the mosque.

The prophet's Holy Mosque in Madinah houses the tomb of the Prophet and is the second most important place in the Islamic world after the holy place in Makkah. The faithful travel to this significant site in ever-increasing numbers from all over the world. The mosque has been extended to provide a dignified place of prayer for all the pilgrims. The new building covers an area 450 m long and 250 m wide, and encloses the mosque extended in 1954 on three sides. 27 courtyards, 18m x 18m, in area, provide the large complex with air and light. The climate of the whole mosque, including the inner courtyards, is controlled by a large air-conditioning plant. The inner courtyards also have convertible roofing that supports the air-conditioning plant in the way that has already been described; they are closed during the day and opened at night.

Two different convertible constructions were developed that are appropriate to the dimensions and different characters of the courtyards. The two large courtyards immediately adjacent to the tomb were shaded by twelve convertible umbrellas. These umbrellas are the product of continuous optimization of the large convertible umbrella and fit quite naturally into the architecture of this religious place. This is achieved partly by the shape of the membrane constructions, which was "found" by self-forming processes, and partly by integrating traditional Islamic architectural and decorative elements into this high-performance design. The ornamentation on the membranes is extremely restrained, and comprehensible in both symbolic and structural terms. The umbrellas move slowly and silently. The folding membranes involve archetypal forms: baldacchinos, chalices, plants, blossoms, white cloths and pilgrims clothing; soft, adaptable

3

4

forms that let in great deal of light. These constructions do not disturb the peaceful gaiety of the place. The faithful are delighted by the cooling shade, and are not cut off from the world, the sky and the symbols of the place.

5

1

The 27 small inner courtyards, 18m x 18m, in the mosque are covered by the "Sliding Domes". These are not light constructions, but convertible constructions that follow an ancient Moroccan tradition. The design of the Sliding Domes also expresses the way in which traditional Islamic architecture has been addressed. Combining this architecture with ultra-modern materials, manufacturing processes and control technology made it possible to develop very adaptable constructions, in terms of both variability and architectural design. The outer and inner shells of the domes are decorated with traditional ornaments, which means that these highly sophisticated technical constructions blend in with the architectural design of the mosque. The most recent technology was used for both the design and the realization of the Sliding Domes. For example, methods were developed while preparing several design variants that draw on the world of three-dimensional Islamic ornament, the so-called Muquarnas (see p. 150).

The Sliding Domes' support structure consists of a horizontal steel girder grid that carries the ring and meridian supports of the dome segment. Four wheel cases are built into the flat steel frame. All the wheels have their own drive mechanism and are controlled by frequency-switched electric motors in such a way that the courtyards can be opened up or closed within a minute. The outer

1 Roof view of the Prophet's holy Mosque in Madinah.

2 Exterior view of the Sliding Domes, with the green dome above the tomb.

3 Alternative design for a lattice shell with underslung membrane.

4 Some of the alternative designs for shades for the 27 small courtyards: toldos and large umbrellas.

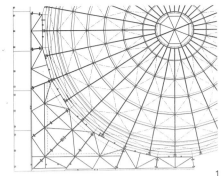

shell of the domes consists of a sandwich construction made up of a carbon-/glass-fibre epoxy laminate with hexagonal ceramic tiles on the outside. The high degree of precision needed to distribute hexagonal tiles on a spherical surface could only be achieved with the aid of digitally controlled machines. These produced forms with milled indentations for each individual tile. The tiles were laid in these indentations on completion and laminated from the rear. The outer shell was decorated in tiles of various shades. The inner shell consists of a timber epoxy laminate covered with a maple veneer. The surface of the panels is lavishly decorated with ornaments carved in Morocco from cedar wood. Special ornament forms are highlighted with mounted Amazonite and gold leaf.

1 Inner shell timber structure, corner area.

2 Mounting the segments of the inner shell.

3 Various fitting stages for the Sliding Domes.

4 The exterior of the inner shell of a dome.

5 Fitting the steel structure.

6 CNC mill creating indentations for the outer shell tiles.

7 Fitting the outer shell.

1 Model of a design alternative for decorating the "Sliding Domes".

2 Detail of the ornamentation in cedar wood, Amazonite stones and gold leaf.

3 A dome sliding into position, inside view.

4 Inside view of the mosque with dome closed.

5 This photograph shows the lavish ornamentation on the domes.

4

5

215

The number of the faithful making the pilgrimage to Madinah is so large that not everyone can find room within the building itself, and so arrive to pray in the great piazza outside the sacred mosque. And so this area too – very large at 200,000 sqm – has to be protected from excessive sunlight with shades, which creates another place for prayer. Additionally, the square has to be well lit as pilgrims are to be found there at all hours of the day or night. To meet these demands, Bodo Rasch's office designed large convertible umbrellas 23 m by 23 m; these have lamps built into them, in the same way as the courtyard umbrellas. The lower umbrella columns were again designed by Dr. Kamal Ismail, chief architect of the mosque.

But lighting a square of this size is still a very complex planning task, and requires an integrated lighting concept. The intention was to provide horizontal illumination for the piazza of 200 lux, as evenly as possible, and using a prescribed grid of possible positions and thus a minimum number of lighting systems. Additionally the facade of the mosque had to be illuminated at an oblique angle, with the intensity of the light increasing from bottom to top. At the same time it was felt to be very important that the lamps and lighting systems were non-glaring.

2

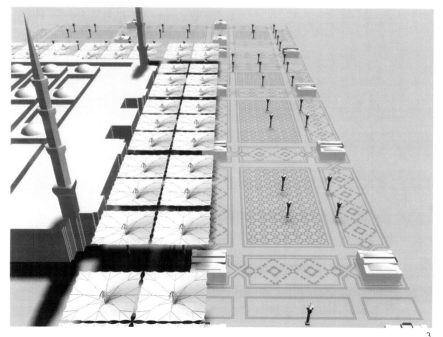

Light and shade in the piazza in front of the Prophet's Holy Mosque in Madinah, 1994:

1 View of the north facade of the mosque.

2 Lighting mast in the piazza.

3 West section of the piazza with umbrellas and lighting masts. (Computer simulation)

3

Traditional lamps produced entirely unsatisfactory results and so four completely new lighting systems were developed in co-operation with Christian Bartenbach of Innsbruck:

1. Illumination for the piazza from lamps that are built into lighting or umbrella masts.
2. Lighting for the piazza from folding reflector system on the "escalator buildings" above the access points to the underground car parks.
3. Low-level lighting from decorative lamps at the corners of the "escalator building".
4. Floodlights to illuminate the facade, also built into the umbrella masts.

1, 2 Views of the north facade with lighting masts and open umbrellas.

3–5 Piazza lamp.

6 View of the illuminated north facade.

3

4

5

6

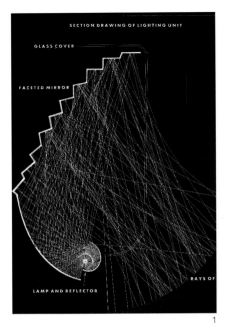

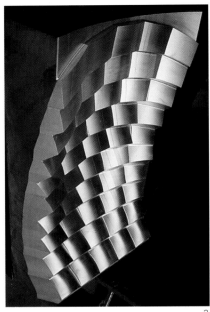

"Spot decomposition" using faceted mirror systems turned out to be the most effective method for all four systems. An aluminium primary reflector unit directs the light from a spot light source on to a secondary reflector, which is subdivided into several free-form surfaces and illuminates a defined area of the piazza. Each free-form surface is calculated to catch the whole of the area to be illuminated. Conversely, an observer from each point sees all light spots, thus optimizing light distribution and reducing dazzle. The human eye is used as the criterion for the distance apart and size of the facet; it must be able to resolve the individual light spots.

The reflector for the "piazza lamps" built into the masts is made up of 50 individual facets. Digitally controlled milling machines mill the free-form areas into an aluminium tool, then an epoxy-carbon-fibre compound is cast from the mould and hardened by heating in a vacuum. The finished carbon-fibre laminate is then lacquered, vapour-plated with aluminium and the surface hardened.

The three-dimensional quality of the mosque facade is brought out by consistently increasing the intensity of the light towards the top of the building. The lamps for this purpose are built into the lighting masts around the mosque. The distribution of light is precisely determined by the geometry and curvature of the reflectors. A counter-reflector surrounding the lamp provides masking in the area in which it is possible to look in to it. Six

1 Drawing of the piazza lamp's beam path.
2 Aluminium base for the piazza lamp reflector.
3 Piazza lamp with bronze case.
4 Prototype for the reflector system.

220

reflector types were developed to adapt to the different distances from and angles to the mosque; these are also made of carbon-fibre laminate vapour-plated with aluminium.

The light source for the reflector system illuminating the access point to the underground car-parks is replaced by a spotlight shining on to a mirrored field with 138 individual facets. Three types of facet compensate for the different light incidence produced by the cone from the spot. As this system is not intended to be visible in the daytime it has a drive mechanism that positions the reflector field only when it is in use.

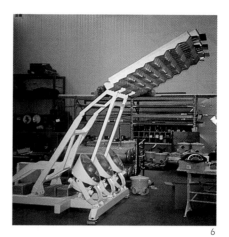

6

5

7

8

The wall lamps in the corners of the underground car-park access building are similar in structure to the piazza lamps, but the facets were replaced by seven rows of conical surfaces. The surfaces that are relevant in terms of lighting technology have something like a hammered structure that scatters the light and makes all the relief in the wall niches glow.

5 Underground car-park access building with reflector system and wall lights, 3-D simulation.

6–8 Steel frame for the reflector system moving into position.

Next page: Time exposure to examine pilgrims' movements during the ritual circling of the Ka'aba (Tawaf) in the courtyard of the Al Harem mosque in Makkah.

Biographies

Frei Otto and Bodo Rasch at the opening of the "Gestalt finden" exhibition in the Villa Stuck in Munich, 1992, on the occasion of the presentation of the Deutscher Werkbund Bayern Prize.

Frei Otto

31.5.1925	Born in Siegmar, Saxony
1943	Advanced school-leaving examination at the Schadow-Schule, Berlin-Zehlendorf. Started to study architecture at the Technische Universität, Berlin
1943–45	War service, prisoner-of-war in Chartres, France, until late 1947, camp architect
1948	Studied in Berlin
1950–51	Study visits to Wright, Mendelson, Saarinen, Mies v.d. Rohe, Neutra, Eames. Studied sociology and urban development at the University of Virginia
1952	Dipl. Ing., free-lance architect in Berlin
1954	Doctorate (Dr. Ing.) "Das hängende Dach" (The suspended roof)
1958–69	Atelier Berlin Türksteinweg
1964–91	Professor and director of the Institute for Lightweight Structures (IL), University of Stuttgart
From 1969	Atelier Frei Otto, Warmbronn

Visiting Professorships

1958	Washington University St. Louis
1959	Hochschule für Gestaltung Ulm
1960	Yale University New Haven
1962	University of California Berkeley
1962	M.I.T. Cambridge
1962	Harvard University Cambridge
1971	Salzburg Summer Academy

Awards and Distinctions

1967	Kunstpreis der Stadt Berlin
1967	Auguste Perret Prize of the Union International des Architectes Prague (with Gutbrod)
1968	Honorary Fellow of the American Institute of Architects
1970	Member of the Akademie der Künste, Berlin
1973	Doctor of Arts and Architecture at the Washington University St. Louis, USA
1974	Thomas Jefferson Medal of the University of Virginia Charlottesville USA
1979	Deutscher Holzbaupreis (with Mutschler)
1980	Honorary Doctor of Science at the University of Bath

1980	Aga Khan Award for Architecture (with Gutbrod) Lahore, Pakistan
1982	Medaille de la recherche et de la technique of the Academie d'Architecture, Paris
1982	Honorary Fellow of the Royal Institute of British Architects
1982	Großer Preis des Bundes deutscher Architekten, Biberach
1983	Member of the Accademia di Archeologica Lettere e Arti Naples
1983	Member of the Academie d'Architecture Paris
1986	Honorary Fellow Institution of Structural Engineers London
1987	Member of the International Academy of Architecture
1989	Sofia International Design Award Osaka
1990	Dr.-Ing. e.h. University of Essen
1990	Honda Prize for Ecotechnology of the Honda Foundation Tokyo
1992	Deutscher Werkbund Bayern Prize, exhibition in the Villa Stuck in Munich
1994	Sustainable Community Solutions Award with Richard Burton(AIA), USA

Buildings

1953–56	Alexandrastiftung Berlin
1955	Bundesgartenschau Kassel
1957	Bundesgartenschau Cologne
1957	Interbau Berlin
1960	Kindergarten and church in Berlin-Schönow (with Bubner)
1962	Deubau, Essen
1963	Internationale Gartenschau Hamburg
1965	Convertible roof in Cannes (for Taillibert)
1967	German Pavilion for Expo Montreal (with Gutbrod, Leonhardt, Kendel et. al.)
1968	Convertible roof Bad Hersfeld
1970	Roof for the Luisenburg in Wunsiedel (with Romberg)
1971	Bundesgartenschau Cologne (with Rasch)
1972	Munich Olympics roof (Behnisch, Leonhardt, Bubner et. al.)
1974	Makkah hotel and conference centre (Gutbrod, Arup)
1975	Aberdeen BP Ceremony Tent (with Arup)
1975	Multihall in Mannheim (Mutschler, Langner, Arup)

1977	Pink Floyd stage roof (with Happold)
1980	Aviary for Hellabrunn Zoo Munich (Gribl, Happold)
1981	Multipurpose hall in Jeddah (with Gutbrod, Henning, Arup, Happold)
from 1982	Hook Park timber school (Burton, Happold, Kanstinger)
1985	Diplomatic-Club Riyadh (with Omrania, Happold, B. Otto, Kanstinger)
1987	Extension for Wilkhahn Bad Münder (with Gestering, Kanstinger)
1990	Ökohouse Berlin (with Kendel, Kanstinger et al.)

Books

Frei Otto as author or editor:

1954	Das hängende Dach, Bauwelt-Verlag
1962	Zugbeanspruchte Konstruktionen, Verlag Ullstein, volume 1
1966	Volume 2
1982	Natürliche Konstruktionen, DVA Stuttgart
1988	Gestaltwerdung, Verlag Rudolf Müller, Arcus 4
1990	Das hängende Dach, reprint with contributions by Rainer Graefe and Christian Schädlich, DVA Stuttgart and Verlag der Kunst Dresden

Authors on Frei Otto

Conrad Roland:	Frei Otto – Spannweiten, Verlag Ullstein, 1965
Ludwig Glaser:	The Work of Frei Otto, Museum of Modern Art, 1972
Philip Drew:	Frei Otto – Form und Konstruktion, Verlag Hatje, 1976
Berthold Burkhardt:	Frei Otto – Schriften und Reden, 1951–83, (ed.) Vieweg-Verlag, 1984
Karin Wilhelm:	Architekten heute – Portrait Frei Otto, Quadriga Verlag, 1985
Stefan Polonyi et. al.:	Der umgekehrte Weg – Frei Otto zum 65. Geburtstag, Verlag Rudolf Müller, Arcus 10, 1990
James Gordon, Edmund Happold et.al.:	Frei Otto. Artigere, Publishers Varese, Italy, 1991

Bodo Rasch

1943	Born in Stuttgart as son of architect Bodo Rasch and painter Lilo Rasch-Naegele
1964-72	Studied architecture at Stuttgart University, graduated with an Engineering Diploma
1967-69	Free-lance worker at the Institut für Leichte Flächentragwerke (IL) at Stuttgart University
1969-72	Worked in Atelier Warmbronn, Prof. Frei Otto's design and development office
1973	Taught at the School of Architecture, University of Texas, Austin, Texas, USA
1974	Pilgrim Accommodation in Muna, urban development competition. Project leader in Frei Otto's team with Sami Angawi
1974	Converted to Islam
1975-79	Founded and developed the Hajj Research Centre at the King Abdel Aziz University, Jeddah, Saudi Arabia, with Sami Angawi
1978-80	Doctoral thesis on the Hajj tent cities at Stuttgart University
from 1980	Architect's office in Stuttgart
1991	Founded SL Sonderkonstruktionen und Leichtbau GmbH
1994	Visiting lecturer at the University of Naples

Awards

1981	Preis der Freunde der Universität Stuttgart
1992	Deutscher Werkbund Bayern Prize
1993	Prize: Best Innovation, International Association for Automation and Robotics in Construction, Houston

Projects

1966	Pneus, studies for the IASS Congress as a free-lance worker at the IL
1968-69	Project director for the new IL Building, 14 Pfaffenwaldring, Stuttgart
1969	Convertible roof for an Olympic stadium, model study

1970–71	Umbrella project director for the Bundesgarten-schau in Cologne (Atelier Warmbronn)
1972–73	Various experimental projects with students in Germany, Italy and the USA
1974–80	Research projects in Saudi Arabia
1981	Mountain Tents project for Muna, with Sami Angawi and Prof. Frei Otto
1982	Arabic Koran edition, with ITS, Cambridge, UK
1982	Sanitary Units for Al Hajj, study for the Hajj tent cities
1983	"Faisal Mosque", design for a mosque in Louisville, KY., USA
1983	Convertible roofing for mobile spectator stands
1984	Convertible roof for Masijid Al Quba, Madinah, Saudi Arabia, realized in 1987
1985	Sails for the Corniche in Jeddah, Saudi Arabia, Design
1985	Finite Element "Climatic Research for convertible Roofs in Saudi Arabia", scientific study
1986–88	Designs for shades for Al Haramein
1987	Finite Elements Simulation of Tawaf Movement, scientific study
1988	Sliding Domes for the Prophet's Holy Mosque, Madinah, Saudi Arabia, design and manufacture of a prototype
1988	"Bodo Rasch – Architect", exhibition at Stuttgart University
1988	Umbrellas for the piazza of the Prophet's Holy Mosque, Madinah, (prototype 10x10m)
1990	Tents for Tuwal Palace
1991–92	Sliding Domes, Madinah, realization
1990–92	Umbrellas (17x18m) for the great courtyards of the Prophet's Holy Mosque, Madinah
1992	Maqam Ibrahim and mobile minbar for Al Harem Al Shareef, Makkah, competition
1992	Deutscher Werkbund Bayern Prize, exhibition in the Villa Stuck, Munich
1993	"Imam Bukhari Educational Complex", Samarkand, Uzbekistan, 1st prize in international competition

Publications

1970   "Tholos", a film about experimental plastic architecture, Abendschau Stuttgart.

1973   "Pneumatics", report on the Delft Symposium on Architectural Design, 1/1973.

1975   "Der Hajj" and "Die Perle des Roten Meeres", illustrated weekly magazine.

1978   "The Pedestrian Movement of Al Hajj", film, 50 min., colour, English/Arabic by Viscom and Hajj Research Centre.

1980   "Zeltstädte des Hajj", IL publication no. 29, monograph, German/English, with Arabic summary, 365 ill.

Notes on the Pictures

Natural Constructions

All the pictures are from the photographic archives of the Institut für Leichte Flächentragwerke, University of Stuttgart. They were taken for research purposes, some were reproduced from books and unfortunately the sources cannot always be identified.

Page 24
Ill. 1:   Terrestrial globe, Zeiss Archive.
          Photograph: Nasa.
Ill. 2:   Star cluster, IL Archive.
Ill. 3:   Vortex, IL Archive.

Page 25
Ill. 1:   Crystals, IL Archive.
Ill. 2:   Basalt, IL Archive.
Ill. 3:   Crystal formation, IL Archive, from:
          1990 Olympus calendar.
Ill. 4:   Clay cracks, IL Archive.

Page 26
Ill. 1:   Rounded-off pebbles, IL Archive.
          Photograph: P. Dombrovskis,
          Granite Beach, South Coast.
Ill. 2:   Travelling dunes, IL Archive,
          B. Baier.
Ill. 3:   Wind erosion, IL Archive, from:
          "Antarktis".
Ill. 4:   Earth towers, IL Archive.
Ill. 5:   Erosion, IL Archive.
Ill. 6:   Rock arch, Rainbow Bridge,
          IL Archive.

Page 27
Ill. 7:   Rock tower, IL Archive,
          from: Geo, 6/52.
Ill. 8:   Mountain folds, IL Archive.
Ill. 9:   Ice arch, IL Archive.

Ill. 10: Cone shapes, IL Archive,
          from: Time-Life.

Page 28
Ill. 1:   Drop, IL Archive,
          student project, 8/1979.
Ill. 2:   Creeks, IL Archive, from: Schwenk,
          Das sensible Chaos.
Ill. 3:   Drop of mercury, IL Archive, K.Bach.
Ill. 4:   Lightning, IL Archive, from:
          Ciba Geigy.
Ill. 5:   Clouds, IL Archive.

Page 29
Ill. 1:   Viscous masses, IL Archive,
          student project, 14/1982.
Ill. 2:   Moon rock, IL Archive. Photograph:
          Mineralogisches Institut Tübingen.
Ill. 3:   Free-floating bubble, IL Archive,
          student project, 8/1979.
Ill. 4:   Bubble cluster, IL Archive,
          Th. Braun, 1976.
Ill. 5:   Icicles, IL Archive, student project,
          8/1979.
Ill. 6:   Stalactites and stalagmites,
          IL Archive, from: Weltwunder der
          Natur, Reval. caused by water drops
          and minerals.

Page 30
Ill. 1:   Microsphere, IL Archive, K. Bach.
Ill. 2:   Cell, IL Archive, A.M. Schmid.
Ill. 4:   Currants, IL Archive, K. Bach.
Ill. 5:   Cell division, IL Archive,
          from: Kessel, Biology.

Page 32
Ill. 1:   Leaf, IL Archive.
Ill. 2:   Grasses, IL Archive.
Ill. 3:   Ramification, IL Archive.
Ill. 4:   Trees, IL Archive, K. Bach.

Page 33
Ill. 1:   Coral, IL Archive, from:
          L. Riefenstahl, Korallengärten.
Ill. 2:   Foetus, 3 months old, IL Archive,
          from: Nilsson, Unser Körper neu
          gesehen, Freiburg, 1974.
Ill. 3:   Sea urchin shell, IL Archive, K. Bach.
Ill. 4:   Tooth formation, IL Archive, from:
          Nilsson, Unser Körper neu gesehen.

Page 34
Ill. 1:   Spider's webs, IL Archive.
Ill. 2:   Spider's web, detail, IL Archive.
          Photograph: E. Kullmann.

Page 35
Ill. 3:   Birds' nests, IL Archive, from:
          K. v. Fritsch, Tiere als Baumeister.
Ill. 4:   Termite city, IL Archive, R. Flößer.
Ill. 5:   Wasps' nest, IL Archive.

Page 36
Path systems, all illustrations: IL Archive.

Page 37
Ill. 1:   Medieval town centre, IL Archive,
          M. Franca, from: Enrico Guidoni,
          Die Europäische Stadt, Milan,
          1979/80.
Ill. 2:   Beach baskets, IL Archive,
          from: Zeit Magazin, 7/89.
Ill. 3:   Settlement, IL Archive, V. Hartkopf.
Ill. 4:   Reed hut, IL Archive,
          from: Institut für
          Auslandsbeziehungen, Stuttgart.
Ill. 5:   Reed hut, IL Archive.
          Photograph: G. Gerster.

Page 38
Ill. 1:   Dry-stone dome,
          IL Archive, H. Drüsedau.

Ill. 2: Pantheon in Rome, IL Archive.
Ill. 3: Clay domes, IL Archive, from the Institut für Auslandsbeziehungen, Stuttgart.
Ill. 4: Ashlar dome, IL Archive.
Ill. 5: Tower foundation in the fortress at Jericho, IL Archive. Photograph: Sheffield Municipal Museum.
Ill. 6: Tower of Babel, vision of 1567, IL Archive.

Page 39
Ill. 1: Arches in a mosque in Cordoba, Spain, IL Archive. Photograph: K. Bach.
Ill. 2: Suspension bridge, IL Archive, Deutsche Fotothek Dresden, from: O. Büttner, E. Hampe: Bauwerk, Tragwerk, Tragstruktur, Stuttgart 1976.
Ill. 3: Fishing nets, IL Archive.
Ill. 4: Iron bridge, IL Archive, from: N. Cossons/B. Trinder: The iron bridge.
Ill. 5: Suspension bridge, IL Archive, Döring, from: Die Inka, Mondoverlag.

Page 40
Ill. 1:1 Project study for a convertible roof for a multimedia stadium for Farbwerke Hoechst. Design: Frei Otto with B. Burkhardt, M. Eekhout, R. Plate, B. Rasch, 1971. Multiple exposure of the opening process in the model, Frei Otto.
Ill. 2: Roof view of the convertible roof over the swimming pool in Regensburg. Drawing: Frei Otto. Architects: J. Schmatz, A. Schmid, H. Mehr, L. Eckel, Atelier Warmbronn, 1970. Constructed by: Stromeyer + Co., Konstanz and Haushahn, Stuttgart, 1971–1972.
Ill. 3: Fold formation, IL Archive, student project, 18/84.

Page 41
Ill. 4: Delft pneumatic bridge. Photograph: Frei Otto.
Ill. 5: Folds in crumpled foil, IL Archive, student project, 16/1984.
Ill. 6: Hot air balloon, IL Archive, from: IWZ.

Page 42
Ill. 1: Suspended chains, IL Archive, Frei Otto.
Ill. 2: Arch in St. Louis, IL Archive.
Ill. 3: Arch of a chain with links, model study Frei Otto, IL.
Ill. 4: Spoil tipping, IL Archive. Photograph: Frei Otto.

Ill. 5: Cistern shape in sand, IL Archive, student project, 13/1989.

Page 43
Ill. 6: Suspended nets with reflection, IL Archive.
Ill. 7: Soap film for a four-point awning, IL Archive.
Ill. 8: Soap film with rope loop, IL Archive.
Ill. 9: Soap film model for a pointed tent with ridges, IL Archive.
Ill. 10: Dome, IL Archive, K. Bach.

Page 44
Ill. 1: Soap film model for a tent, IL Archive, student project, 10/88.
Ill. 2: Soap film in wind, IL Archive, student project, 21/1978.
Ill. 3: Yacht, IL Archive, E. Haug.
Ill. 4: Three-dimensional net, IL Archive, student project, 26/1985.

Page 46
Ill. 1: Vortex, IL Archive, S. Gaß.
Ill. 2: Funnel in sand, IL Archive, student project, 13/1989.
Ill. 3: Cones and craters, IL Archive.

Page 47
Ill. 4: Surface occupied by spheres, IL Archive, from: Kepes, Struktur in Kunst und Wissenschaft.
Ill. 5: Bubbles, IL Archive, student project, 12/1979.
Ill. 6: Specks of fat , IL Archive, K. Bach.
Ill. 7: Direct path system, IL Archive, student project, 7/1988.
Ill. 8: Minimal path system, IL Archive.
Ill. 9: Thread model, IL Archive, Marek Kolodziejczyk.
Ill. 10: Cracks in concrete, IL Archive.

Page 48
Ill. 1: Cells, IL Archive.
Ill. 2: Soap bubble, IL Archive, student project, 11/1976.
Ill. 3: Electrical discharge, IL Archive, Lichtenberg.
Ill. 4: Branching structure, IL Archive.
Ill. 5: Computer simulation of a branching structure, IL Archive.
Ill. 6: Internal reinforcement of a pneumatic construction, model with plaster cast, IL Archive, student project, 9/1985.

Page 49
Ill. 7: Fibre network of a cell, IL Archive.
Ill. 8: Sea-lion, IL Archive, K. Bach.
ill. 9: Fibre formation in viscous liquid, IL Archive, student project, 6/89.

Ill. 10: Radiolaria, IL Archive, J. G. Helmcke, Berlin.
Ill. 11: Bubbles, IL Archive, student project, 13/1979.

Page 50
Ill. 1: Detail from a three-dimensional thread model, IL Archive, Marek Kolodziejczyk.
Ill. 2: Threads drawn from a plastic mass, IL Archive, student project, 3/1989.
Ill. 3: Bone interior, IL Archive, K. Bach.
Ill. 4: Folds in a shrunken apple, IL Archive, student project, 12/1984.
Ill. 5: Pollen, IL Archive. Photograph: E.Kullmann.
Ill. 6: Bone structure, IL Archive, K. Bach.

Page 51
Ill. 1: Horizontal drop of mercury, IL Archive, K. Bach.
Ill. 2: Frozen soap bubble, IL Archive.
Ill. 3: Net pneumatic structure, IL Archive, student project, 12/1978.

Experiments

Page 55
Ill. 1: Stability experiments with a tilting turntable, Frei Otto with Bodo Rasch, 1993. Photograph: Frei Otto.

Page 56
Ill. 1: Apparatus for soap film experiments in the Villa Stuck, Munich, 1992. Photograph: SL Archive, Gabriela Heim, IL.
Ill. 2: Apparatus for producing pneumatic constructions, Villa Stuck, Munich, 1992. Photograph: SL Archive, Gabriela Heim, IL.

Page 57
Ill. 3: Tilting turntables to investigate the stability of masonry buildings, Villa Stuck, Munich, 1992. Photograph: SL Archive, Gabriela Heim, IL.
Ill. 4: Models made of plaster bandages, Frei Otto in Villa Stuck, Munich, 1992. Photograph: SL. Archive: Gabriela Heim, IL.
Ill. 5: Discharge funnel and spoil cone in dry sand, student project at IL, 13/1989.

Page 58
Ill. 1: Soap film in wind. Photograph: IL, 1978.
Ill. 2: Soap film model of a pointed tent, student project at IL, 21/1985. Photograph: IL Archive.

232

Ill. 3: Soap film machine at the IL with soap film model in parallel light and camera. Photograph: IL Archive, Klaus Bach.

Page 59
Ill. 4: Four-point awning soap film. Photograph: IL Archive, Klaus Bach.
Ill. 5: Soap film model: spiral surface with flat plate, student project at IL, 1/1983.
Ill. 6: Soap film model in a circle with vertical lamella, student project at IL, 3/1885. Photograph: IL Archive.

Page 60
Ill.1, 2: Comparative examination of a pneumatically formed plaster model with a suspended net model, student project at IL, 5/1975.
Ill. 3: Soap film on a dumb-bell plan. Photograph: IL, Frei Otto, 1963.
Ill. 4: Project study for roofing a town in Alberta, Canada. Architects and engineers: Arni Fullerton, Edmonton Canada, Atelier Frei Otto, Warmbronn, Happold Office, Bath, 1981. Photograph: Frei Otto.

Page 61
Ill. 5: Plaster model, Bodo Rasch, Jose Mirafuentes, 1996. Photograph: IL Archive.

Page 62
Ill. 1: Suspended model for the study of gravity suspended roofs, student project at IL, 12/1983.
Ill. 2: Suspended model (with mirror image) of a square-mesh suspended net made up of four triangular segments, student project at IL, 12/1983.
Ill. 3: Suspended model for the construction of a pagoda roof, Atelier Frei Otto, Warmbronn, B. Dreher, 1978.

Page 63
Ill. 4,5 Plaster bandage models. Frei Otto, 1992. Photograph: Atelier Frei Otto, Warmbronn.
Ill. 6: Suspended model to find the shape of groin vaulting, student project at IL, 4/1985.

Page 64
Ill. 1: Discharge funnels and spoil cones in sand, student project at IL, 13/1989. Photographs: IL Archive.

Page 65
Ill. 2-4: Discharge funnels and spoil cones in sand, student project at IL, 9/1989. Photographs: IL Archive.

Ill. 5,6 Funnels and spoil cones in sand. Photographs: Frei Otto.

Page 66
Ill. 1,2,3: Drawings, Frei Otto, 1993.
Ill. 4: Stability experiment on a dome with skylight as part of a competition for extending Imam Bukhari's tomb mosque in Samarkand (see chapter on shells), Atelier Warmbronn, Architekturbüro Bodo Rasch, 1993. Photograph: Ingrid Otto.

Page 67
Ill. 5: Stability experiments on a tall brick structure with a square ground plan, Atelier Warmbronn, Frei Otto with Ingrid Otto, Dietmar Otto, Christine Otto-Kanstinger. Photographs: Ingrid Otto.

Page 68, 69
Ill. 1: Thread model with water lamella and open branching. Photograph: IL Archive, Klaus Bach.
Ill. 2-,7: Thread model built by Marek Kolodziejczyk at IL.

Page 70
Ill. 1: Minimal path system. Model: Frei Otto. Photograph: Frei Otto.
Ill. 2,3: Minimal path systems, student project at IL, 16/1985. Photographs: IL Archive.
Ill. 4: Minimal path system, student project, at IL, 2/85. Photograph: IL Archive.

Page 71
Sketches of model structure for area occupation simulation apparatus, Frei Otto, 1993.

Literature: IL 18 Soap films; IL 25 Experiments; IL 39 Eda Schaur: Ungeplante Siedlungen; Frei Otto: Natürliche Konstruktionen, DVA Stuttgart, 1982.

Tent Constructions

Page 73
Ill. 1: 'Membrane forms' study model. Authors: Atelier Frei Otto, Warmbronn, Christine Otto-Kanstinger, Gisela Stromeyer, Mark Heller, 1986.

Page 74
Ill. 1: Kirghiz yurts. Photograph: IL Archive, from: Dar and Naumann, Die Kirgisen im afghanischen Pamir, 1978.

Ill. 2: North American Indian tepee. Photograph: IL Archive.

Page 75
Ill. 3: "Neige et Rocs" pavilion at the Schweizerische Landesausstellung in Lausanne, 1964. Architects: Saugey, Schierle, Geneva, Frei Otto. Ingenieure: Froidveau, Weber, Lausanne. Execution: L. Stromeyer und Co., Konstanz. Photograph: Atelier Warmbronn.
Ill. 4: Pavilion at the Bundesgartenschau in Cologne, 1957. Architects and engineers: Frei Otto with E. Bubner, S. Lohs, D.R. Frank. Execution: L. Stromeyer und Co., Konstanz. Photograph: IL Archive, Atelier Warmbronn.
Ill. 5: Soap film model of a four-point awning. Model: Frei Otto, 1960. Photograph: Atelier Warmbronn.
Ill. 6: Four-point awning as a music pavilion at the 1955 Bundesgartenschau. Architect: Frei Otto. Execution: L. Stromeyer und Co., Konstanz. Photograph: Atelier Warmbronn.

Page 76
Ill. 1: Soap film model of an arch-supported membrane, study at the IL, Klaus Bach, 1986. Photograph: IL Archive.
Ill. 2: Soap-film model of a membrane surface with rope loop, student project at IL, 5/1991. Photograph: IL Archive, Klaus Bach.
Ill. 3: Computer simulation of a membrane surface with rope loop. Comparative study: S. Schanz, IL and Joachim Bahndorf, Institut für angewandte Geodäsie im Bauwesen, University of Stuttgart, 1992. Photograph: IL Archive.

Page 77
Ill. 4: Night photograph of the great wave hall at the International Garden Show in Hamburg, 1963. Architects: Frei Otto with H. Habermann, Ch. Hertling, J. Koch, 1963. Execution: L. Stromeyer und Co., Konstanz. Photograph: Atelier Warmbronn.
Ill. 5: Soap film model of a parallel wave tent, student project at IL, 15/1985. Photograph: IL Archive, Klaus Bach.

Page 78
Ill. 1-3: Entrance arch to the 1957 Bundesgartenschau in Cologne. Architects and engineers: Frei Otto with E. Bubner, S. Lohs, D.R. Frank.

Execution: L. Stromeyer und Co., Konstanz. Photograph: Atelier Frei Otto, Warmbronn.

Page 79

Ill. 4,6   Humped tent at the 1957 Bundesgartenschau in Cologne. Architects and engineers: Frei Otto with E. Bubner. S. Lohs, D.R. Frank. Execution: E. Stromeyer and Co., Konstanz. Photograph: Atelier Frei Otto, Warmbronn.

Ill. 5:   Soap film, distorted into a so-called hump by elastic lamellas, student project at IL, 11/1977. Photograph: IL Archive.

Page 80, 81

Ill. 1,4   Dance Fountain in Cologne. Architects and engineers: Frei Otto with E Bubner, S. Lohs, D.R. Frank, 1957. Execution: E. Stromeyer and Co., Konstanz. Photograph: IL Archive, Atelier Frei Otto, Warmbronn.

Ill. 1;   Soap film model of the star wave, Cologne Dance Fountain. Photographs: IL, Frei Otto.

Ill. 2,3,5:   Star-wave tent over gardens in Thowal, Saudi Arabia. Architects: Bodo Rasch with J. Bradatsch, B. Gawenat, H. Voigt, 1991. Engineers: Mayr+Ludescher, Stuttgart. Execution: Koit high-tex, Rimsting.

Ill. 2:   Computer simulation.

Ill. 3:   Tulle model. Photographs: SL Archive.

Page 82, 83

Ill. 1:   Cross-wave tents at the International Garden Show in Hamburg, 1963. Architects: Frei Otto with H. Habermann, Ch. Hertling, J. Koch, 1963. Execution: E. Stromeyer and Co., Konstanz. Photograph: Atelier Frei Otto, Warmbronn.

Ill. 2:   Great wave hall at the International Garden Show in Hamburg, 1963. Architects: Frei Otto with H. Habermann, Ch. Hertling, J. Koch, 1963. Execution: E. Stromeyer and Co., Konstanz. Photograph: Atelier Frei Otto, Warmbronn.

Ill. 3:   Reception tent in the beach complex tent in Thowal, Saudi Arabia. Architects: Bodo Rasch with J. Bradatsch, B. Gawenat, H. Voigt, 1991. Engineers: Mayr + Ludescher, Stuttgart. Execution: Koit high-tex, Rimsting. Photographs: SL Archive.

Page 84

Ill. 1–3:   Stand covering at the Thowal beach complex sports field. Architects: Bodo Rasch with J. Bradatsch, B. Gawenat, H. Voigt, 1991. Engineers: Mayr + Ludescher, Stuttgart. Execution: Koit high-tex, Rimsting. Photographs: SL Archive.

Page 85

Ill. 3,5:   Humped ceremonial tent to Elizabeth II at Dyce near Aberdeen, Scotland, 1975. Architects: Design Research Unit, London, Frei Otto with E. Bubner, Peter Stromeyer und Co., Konstanz. Engineers: Ove Arup and Partners, London. Photographs: Atelier Frei Otto, Warmbronn, IL Archive.

Ill. 4:   Design model of a festival tent for Elizabeth II in Sullom Voe, Shetland Islands, for the opening of the new oil refinery. Architects: Frei Otto with H. Doster, J. Fritz, N. Stone, H. Theune. Engineers: Happold Office, Bath, design 1981, not executed. Photograph: Atelier Frei Otto, Warmbronn.

Page 86

Ill. 1–4:   Sarabhai tent. Design: Atelier Frei Otto, Warmbronn, 1973, with Ewald Bubner, Matthias Banz, Jean Goedert, Fürst Alf von Lieven, Georgios Papakostas, Geoffrey Wright. Commissioned by: Gautahm and Gira Sarabhai, Sarabhai International, Ahmedabad, India. Manufacturers: Sarabhai and Ballonfabrik Augsburg. Photographs: IL Archive.

Page 87

Ill. 5,6:   Study model of a painted tent, designed as a pavilion for the "Golden Eye" exhibition (joint India-USA project with international designers). Cooper-Hewitt Museum, New York. Design: Atelier Frei Otto, Warmbronn, 1985. Painting: Bettina Otto. Photograph: Atelier Frei Otto, Warmbronn.

Ill. 7:   Painted round tent, contribution to "Golden Eye". Architects: Frei Otto with J. Bradatsch, 1985. The painting was done in India and based on traditional ornament. Photograph: Atelier Frei Otto, Warmbronn.

Page 88, 89

Ill. 1–3:   Heart Tent at the Diplomatic Club in Riyadh, Saudi Arabia, known as the Tuwaiq Palace. Architects and engineers: OhO Joint Venture (Frei Otto, T. Happold, Omrania), 1985. Execution: 1986-1988. Painting: Bettina Otto. Photographs: 1,3: B. Kaser, SL; 2: Frei Otto.

Pages 90, 91

Ill. 1–3:   Diplomatic Club in Riyadh, Saudi Arabia, known as the Tuwaiq Palace. Architects and engineers: OhO Joint Venture (Frei Otto, T. Happold, Omrania), 1985. Execution: 1986-1988. Painting: Bettina Otto. Photographs: Frei Otto.

Literature: IL 16 Tents; IL 18 Soap Films; IL 25 Experiments; Frei Otto: Natürliche Konstruktionen, DVA Stuttgart, 1982. Conrad Roland: Frei Otto – Spannweiten, Verlag Ullstein, 1965. Philip Drew: Frei Otto, Hatje, 1976.

Net Constructions

Page 93

Illustration: German Pavilion rope net at the 1967 Montreal World Fair. Architects: Rolf Gutbrod, Frei Otto, Hermann Kendel, Hermann Kies, Larry Medlin. Engineers: Leonhardt-Andrä, H. Egger, Stuttgart. Execution planning: roof: IL, Frei Otto, E. Haug, L. Medlin, J. Schilling et. al. Execution: E. Stromeyer and Co., Konstanz. Photograph: IL Archive.

Page 94

Ill. 1,2:   "Neige et Rocs" pavilion for the 1963 Schweizerische Landesausstellung in Lausanne. Architects: M. Saugey, Geneva. Engineers: Froidveau + Weber, Lausanne. Constructional advice: Frei Otto with Romberg, Röder, Hertling. Manufacturers: Stromeyer und Co., Konstanz. Photograph: Atelier Frei Otto, Warmbronn.

Page 95

Ill. 3:   Finding-form study for the support of textile membranes and rope nets using a rope loop, the so-called eye. This model gave Frei Otto and Rolf Gutbrod the design idea for the German pavilion at Expo 1967 in Montreal. Design and model: Atelier Frei Otto, Berlin with Larry Medlin, 1965. Photograph: Atelier Frei Otto, Warmbronn.

Ill. 4: Rope net for the German Pavilion in Montreal, Stuttgart-Vaihingen, 1966. Architects: Institut für Leichte Flächentragwerke, Frei Otto with E. Haug, L. Medlin, G. Minke et. al. Engineers: Leonhardt und Andrä, Stuttgart. Photograph: Atelier Frei Otto, Warmbronn.

Page 96–99
Ill. Rope net for the German pavilion at the Montreal World Fair, 1967. Architects: Rolf Gutbrod, Frei Otto, Hermann Kendel, Hermann Kies, L. Medlin, J. Schilling, B. Burkhardt et. al. Execution: E. Stromeyer and Co., Konstanz. Photograph: Atelier FreiOtto, Warmbronn.

Page 100, 101
Ill.: Experimental building for the German Pavilion in Montreal, Stuttgart-Vaihingen, 1966. Architects: Institut für Leichte Flächentragwerke, Frei Otto with E. Haug, L. Medlin, G Minke et. al. Engineers: Leonhardt und Andrä, Stuttgart. Photographs: IL Archive, Atelier Frei Otto, Warmbronn.

Pages 102–105
Ill.: Institut für Leichte Flächentrag-werke, University of Stuttgart at Vaihingen, built 1967–1969. Architects: Frei Otto with Bodo Rasch, L. Medlin, B. Burkhardt, G. Minke, F. Kugel. Engineers: Leonhardt und Andrä, Stuttgart. Photographs: IL Archive, Atelier Frei Otto, Warmbronn.

Page 106, 107
Ill.: Olympic roofs in Munich, 1972. Architects and engineers: Behnisch und Partner, Frei Otto with IL, E. Bubner, J. Hennicke, B. Burkhardt, F. Kugel, H.J. Schock et. al. Leonhardt und Andrä. Photographs: IL Archive, Atelier Frei Otto, Warmbronn.

Page 108, 109
Ill.: Aviary in the zoo at Munich-Hellabrunn. Architects: Jörg Gribl with Atelier Frei Otto, Warmbronn. Engineers: Happold Office, Bath. Execution: E. Stromeyer and Co., Konstanz. Photographs: 1,4: S. Schanz; 2,3: Frei Otto.

Page 110
Ill.: Sports hall in King Abdul Aziz University, Jeddah, Saudi Arabia.

Architects: Frei Otto, Rolf Gutbrod with Henning, Kendel, Riede. Engineers: Happold Office with E. Happold, Bath, design c.1975, completed 1980. Photographs: IL Archive, Atelier Frei Otto, Warmbronn.

Page 111
Ill. 1: Model study for a rope net cooling tower in minimum surface shape. Design and model building: Atelier Frei Otto, Warmbronn, 1974. Photograph: Frei Otto.
Ill. 2: Soap film model of a catenoid, study at the IL. Photograph: IL Archive.
Ill. 3: Model study for a suspension building. Design and model building: Frei Otto. Photograph: Frei Otto.

Literature: IL 8 Nets in Nature and Technology; IL 16 Tents; IL 18 Soap films; IL 25 Experiments; Frei Otto: Natürliche Konstruktionen, DVA Stuttgart, 1982. Conrad Roland: Frei Otto – Spannweiten, Verlag Ullstein, 1965. Philip Drew: Frei Otto, Hatje, 1976.

Pneumatic Constructions

Page 113
Ill. 1: Plaster study model of an air hall, Frei Otto, 1960. Photograph: Frei Otto.

Page 114
Ill. 1: Montgolfier balloons, historical photograph. Photograph: IL Archive.
Ill. 2: Hot air balloons. Photograph: IL Archive.

Page 115
Ill. 3: Air hall over a satellite aerial in Raisting. Design and manufacture: Birdair Structures. Photograph: Frei Otto.
Ill. 4: F.W. Lanchester's Patent, from: Thomas Herzog: Pneumatische Konstruktionen, Hatje, 1976.

Page 116
Ill. 1: Industrial plant with three pneumatically supported domes. Design: Frei Otto, 1958. Photograph: Frei Otto.
Ill. 2: Spherical pneumatic structure as a bulk material store. Design: Frei Otto, 1960. Photograph: Frei Otto.
Ill. 3: Exhibition pavilion for the 1958 Floriade in Rotterdam. Design: Frei Otto, 1958. Photograph: Frei Otto.

Page 117
Ill. 4: Plaster study for an air hall with internal drainage, IL, 1966. Photograph: Frei Otto.
Ill. 5: Tied-in plaster model, student project at IL, 9/1985. Photograph: IL Archive.
Ill. 6: Tied-in soap bubble model, IL. Photograph: IL Archive.

Page 118
Ill. 1: Soap foam, IL study. Photograph: Thomas Braun, IL.
Ill. 2: Soap bubble model, IL. Photograph: Klaus Bach.
Ill. 3: Pentadome exhibition pavilion, 1958. Architects: Birdair Structures. Photograph: IL Archive.

Page 119
Ill. 4: Exhibition pavilion at the 1964 World Fair in New York. Design: Victor Lundy. Manufacture: Birdair Structures. Photograph: IL Archive.
Ill. 5: US pavilion at Expo 1970 in Osaka. Architects: Davis, Brody, de Harak Chermayeff, Geismar. Engineers: Geiger und Berger, New York. Photograph: IL Archive.

Page 120, 121
Ill. 1–3: "City in Antarctica". Architects: Atelier Frei Otto, Warmbronn, Frei Otto and Ewald Bubner with Kenzo Tange and URTEC, Tokyo. Engineers: Ove Arup and Partners, London, 1971. Design not realized. Photographs: Frei Otto.
Ill. 4, 5: Design for roofing a city in Alberta, Canada, 1/1980. Architects and engineers: Arni Fullerton, Edmonton, Canada, Happold Office, Bath, England, Atelier Frei Otto, Warmbronn. Photographs: Frei Otto.

Page 122
1 Low pressure pneumatic structure as a projection wall, 1966. Architects: B.-F. Romberg, Frei Otto. Manufacture: E. Stromeyer and Co., Konstanz. Photograph: Atelier Frei Otto, Warmbronn.

Page 123
Ill.: Project studies Airfish 1,2,3, 1978, 1979, 1988. Designs: Atelier Frei Otto, Warmbronn, Frei Otto with R. Barthel, H. Hoster, J. Fritz, Christine Otto-Kanstinger. Happold Office, Bath, E. Happold with

I. Lidell and Aeronautical College Cranfield Institute of Technology. Photograph: Atelier Frei Otto, Warmbronn.

Page 124
Ill. 1:   Free-floating soap bubble, student project at IL, 11/1976. Photograph: IL Archive.
Ill. 2:   Drops of mercury. Photograph:Klaus Bach, IL.
Ill. 3:   Living cell. Photograph: A.M. Schmid. IL

Page 125
Ill. 4:   Series of soap bubbles. Photograph: Th. Braun, IL.
Ill. 5:   Radiolaria. Photograph: Johann Gerhard, helmcke, Berlin.
Ill. 6:   Balloon strung with rope net. Photograph: Klaus Bach, IL.
Ill. 7:   Soap film with net. Photograph: hector, IL, 1974.

Literature: IL 9 Pneumatic structures in nature and technology; IL 15 Air hall handbook; IL 18 Soap films; IL 25 Experiments; Frei Otto: Natürliche Konstruktionen, DVA Stuttgart, 1982. Conrad Roland: Frei Otto – Spannweiten, Verlag Ullstein, 1965. Thomas herzog: Pneumatische Konstruktionen, hatje, 1976.

Suspended Constructions

Page 127
Ill.:   Suspension model in square-mesh chain netting, Atelier Frei Otto, Warmbronn, Frei Otto with Birgit Dreher, 1978.

Pages 128, 129
Ill. 1:   Suspension models to study the shape of Asian roofs, student project at IL, 14/1983. Photographs: ILArchive.
Ill. 2:   Suspension models to study the shape of Asian roofs, student project at IL, 14/1983. Photographs: IL Archive.
Ill. 3-7:   hotel and conference centre in Makkah, Saudi Arabia. Architects: Atelier Frei Otto, Warmbronn, Büro Gutbrod, Stuttgart with A. Claar, h. Kendel. Engineers: Ove Arup and Partners, London. Photographs: Atelier Frei Otto, Warmbronn.

Page 130
Ill. 1, 3: Medical academy in Ulm. Architect: Atelier Frei Otto, Berlin, 1965. Design

not executed. Photograph: Frei Otto.
Ill. 2,4:   Extension structure for the Fachhochschule in Ulm. Architect: Atelier Frei Otto, Berlin, 1965. Architects: Frei Otto, Guther und Partner, Ulm, 1991. Engineers: happold Office, Bath. Garden designers: Luz und Partner, Stuttgart. Design not executed. Photograph: Atelier Frei Otto, Warmbronn.

Page 131
Ill.:   Wilkhahn extension building in Bad Münder. Architects: Atelier Frei Otto, Warmbronn, Frei Otto with Christine Otto-Kanstinger, Planungsgruppe Gestering, Bremen, h. Gestering. Engineers: Stratman, Speich und hinkes. Execution 1987.

Page 132, 133
Ill. 1,2:   Competition design for roofing the stand at the Berlin Olympic Stadium, 1969. Architects: Atelier Frei Otto, Warmbronn, Büro Gutbrod. Engineers: Ove Arup + Partners, London, happold Office, Bath, Oleiko, Rice, Thornsteinn. Not executed. Photograph: Frei Otto.
Ill. 3,4:   Competition design for stand roofing for the Neckar- or Gottlieb-Daimler-Stadion in Stuttgart. Engineers: Ove Arup + Partners, London, happold Office, Bath, Oleiko, Rice, Thornsteinn. Not executed. Photograph: Frei Otto.

Literature: IL 17 The work of Frei Otto and his team, IL 25 Experiments, Frei otto: Natürliche Konstruktionen, DVA Stuttgart, 1982. Conrad Roland: Frei Otto – Spannweiten, Verlag Ullstein, 1965.

Arches, Vaults, Shells

Page 135
Ill. 1:   New design for the hopfenmarkt and the nave of the Nicolaikirche in hamburg. Architects: Atelier Frei Otto, Warmbronn. Design 1992, not executed. Photograph: Frei Otto.

Page 136
Ill. 1,2:   Suspended chains. Model and photograph: Frei Otto.

Page 137
Ill. 3,4:   Models to demonstrate the inversion of a catenary to form the pressure line of an arch, student project, 19/86. Photographs: IL Archive.
Ill. 5:   Reconstruction of Antoni Gaudi suspension model for the Colonia Güell church. Model built by: IL, I. Graefe, Frei Otto, J. Tomlow, A. Walz. Photograph: IL Archive.
Ill. 6:   Chain net suspension models. Studies at the University of California in Berkeley during Frei Otto's visiting professorship, 1962. Photograph: IL Archive.
Ill. 7:   Suspension model to find form for groin vaults, student project at IL, 4/1985. Photograph: IL Archive.
Ill. 8:   Suspension model to find the form of cross vaults. The photograph has been turned through 180° to show the vault form, student project at IL, 4/1985. Photograph: IL Archive.

Page 138
Ill. 1-5:   Lattice shell at DEUBAU in Essen. Architects and engineers: Frei Otto with B.F. Romberg, E. Pietsch, J. Koch, 1962. Photographs: IL Archive, Atelier Frei Otto, Warmbronn.

Page 139
Ill. 6,7:   Design model for a metal bar lattice shell as a pavilion in Volkspark Rehberg, Berlin, 1969. Architects: Frei Otto with B. F. Romberg, E. Bubner, 1969. Photographs: IL Archive, Atelier Frei Otto, Warmbronn.
Ill. 8:   Study model of the transformation of a suspended net into a lattice shell made of round wooden bars. Model built by: students at Frei Otto's Salzburg Summer Academy master class, 1970. Photograph: IL Archive.

Page 140-142
Ill.:   Mannheim lattice shell. Architects: Mutschler and Langner with Frei Otto, 1971. Engineers: Ove Arup and Partners with happold, Dickson, Ealy et. al. Photographs: IL Archive, Atelier Frei Otto, Warmbronn.

Page 143
Ill. 1:   Suspension model, student project at IL, 6/1979. Photograph: IL Archive.

Ill. 2:   King's Office (KO), Council of
           Ministers (COM), Majlis al Shura
           (MAS), (KOCOMMAS), Riyadh,
           Saudi Arabia. Architects:
           Rolf Gutbrod, Frei Otto, Berlin,
           Stuttgart, 1979. Engineers: Happold
           Office, Bath, Ove Arup and Partners,
           London. Hexagonal shell (diameter
           70 m) on branched supports, above
           the inner courtyard with cabinet
           room and inner garden (COM).
           Design not executed. Photograph:
           Frei Otto.

Page 144
Ill.:   Design model for the competition for
           the German pavilion at the Seville
           World Fair, 1992. Competition 1990
           (2nd prize, not built). Architects:
           Atelier Frei Otto, Warmbronn,
           Frei Otto, Ingrid Otto,
           Christine Otto-Kanstinger et. al.
           Engineers: Happold Office, Bath.
           Model photographs: Frei Otto.

Page 145
Ill.:   New design for the Hopfenmarkt and
           the nave of the Nicolaikirche in
           Hamburg. Architects: Atelier
           Frei Otto, Warmbronn. Design 1992,
           not executed. Photograph: Frei Otto.

Page 146–149
Competition design for extending Imam
Bukhari's tomb mosque with adjacent new
university building in Samarkand. Architects:
Bodo Rasch with N. Stone, Saleem Bukhari,
Kamal Schorachmedow, A. Purohit, Atelier Frei
Otto, Warmbronn; Frei Otto, Ingrid Otto,
Christine Otto-Kanstinger, 1993.

Page 146
Ill. 1:   Competition drawing, Architekturbüro
           Bodo Rasch, 1993.
Ill. 2:   From "Samarkand: a museum in the
           open", V. Bulatova, G. Shishkina,
           N. Vasilkin, Tashkent, 1986.

Page 147
Ill. 3:   This series of experiments with the
           tilting turntable shows the behaviour
           of the dome with skylight under
           horizontal load, Atelier Frei Otto,
           Warmbronn; Frei Otto with Ingrid Otto,
           Christine Otto-Kanstinger,
           Dietmar Otto. Photographs: Atelier
           Frei Otto, Warmbronn.

Page 148
Ill. 1:   Section and ground plan of the dome.
           Drawing: Architecturbüro
           Bodo Rasch.

Ill. 2:   Model of the dome form with skylight,
           Atelier Frei Otto, Warmbronn.
Ill. 3:   Drawing: Frei Otto.

Page 149
Ill. 4–6: Design drawings:
           Architecturbüro Bodo Rasch.

Page 150, 151
Ill. 1:   Muqarnas above the entrance to the
           Sheikh Lutfallah mosque, 1602–1618.
           Photograph: SL Archive, from:
           Henri Stierlin: Isfahan, Atlantis, 1976.
Ill. 2–7: Designs for muqarnas, preliminary
           designs for the "Sliding Domes"
           project, see pp. 210–215. Architects:
           Bodo Rasch with R. Bühler,
           B. Gawenat, 1990.
Ill. 2:   Isometric drawings and photographs:
           SL Archive.

Page 152, 153
Ill.:   Historical examination of the
           architecture of the Pantheon in
           Rome. Institut für Leichte Flächen-
           tragwerke, from: "Zur Geschichte des
           Konstruierens", edited by
           Rainer Graefe, DVA Stuttgart, 1989.
           Photographs: IL Archive.

Page 154, 155
Ill.:   Reconstruction of Gaudí's
           suspension model for the
           "Colonia Güell" church, Institut für
           Leichte Flächentragwerke, R. Graefe,
           J. Tomlow, A. Walz, Frei Otto, IL, from:
           IL 34, Jos Tomlow, "Das Modell".

Literature: IL 10 Lattice domes, IL 13 Mannheim
multi-hall, IL 25 Experiments, IL 34 Gaudi, the
model. Frei Otto: Natürliche Konstruktionen,
DVA Stuttgart, 1982. Conrad Roland: Frei Otto
– Spannweiten, Verlag Ullstein, 1965. Philip
Drew: Frei Otto, Hatje, 1976. "Zur Geschichte
des Konstruierens", ed. Rainer Graefe, DVA
Stuttgart, 1989.

Branched Constructions

Page 157
Ill. 1:   Branched construction as track for
           the magnet express train. Architects
           and engineers: Atelier Frei Otto,
           Warmbronn and Happold Office, Bath:
           Frei Otto, Christine Otto-Kanstinger,
           Ingrid Otto, Dietmar Otto,
           Edmund Happold, Michael Dickson,
           Rüdiger Lutz, 1991/92, not executed.
           Photograph: Atelier Frei Otto,
           Warmbronn.

Page 158–160
Sketches by Frei Otto, 1992.

Page 161
Ill. 1:   Preliminary design for an exhibition
           hall, model. Frei Otto's students
           during a seminar at Yale University,
           1960. Photograph: Atelier Frei Otto,
           Warmbronn.
Ill. 2:   Branched rod construction,
           student project at IL, 12/79.
           Photograph: IL Archive.

Page 162
Ill. 1:   Model of a branched support
           structure, student project at IL, 1984.
           Photograph: Atelier Frei Otto,
           Warmbronn.
Ill. 2:   Study model using rubber bands to
           establish minimalized detours,
           Frei Otto, 1983.
Ill. 3:   Pneumatically tensioned branch
           structure, sculpture by Frei Otto.

Page 163
Ill. 4:   Branched construction as support
           for a hexagonal lattice shell in the
           KOCOMMAS project, Riyadh,
           Saudi Arabia. Architects:
           Rolf Gutbrod, Frei Otto, Berlin,
           Stuttgart, 1980. Engineers:
           Happold Office, Bath, Ove Arup and
           Partners, London. The building was
           not completed.
Ill. 5:   Drawing by Frei Otto, 1980.
Ill. 6   This model made of steel springs was
           built in Atelier Frei Otto, Warmbronn in
           1983 to study bracing forces in
           tension-loaded constructions.

Page 164, 165
Ill: Designs for a new track for the
           German magnet train system.
           Architects and engineers: Atelier
           Frei Otto, Warmbronn and
           Happold Office, Bath: Frei Otto,
           Christine Otto-Kanstinger,
           Ingrid Otto, Dietmar Otto,
           Edmund Happold, Michael Dickson,
           Rüdiger Lutz, 1991/92, not executed.
           Photograph: Atelier Frei Otto,
           Warmbronn.

Literature: Frei Otto: Natürliche Konstruktionen,
DVA Stuttgart, 1982.

Energy and Environmental Technology

Page 167
Ill.:   Model for the moving cover for
           harmful waste dumps, design 1994.

Architects: Frei Otto with Ingrid Otto, Christine Otto-Kanstinger, Bodo Rasch with B. Gawenat, S. Greiner. Engineers: E. happold, Bath. Photograph: Atelier Frei Otto, Warmbronn.

Page 168, 169
Drawings and photographs from IL 11 Light structures and energy technology.
Ill. 2:   Model study under-water rainwater reservoir, Frei Otto, 1967.
Ill. 3:   Cable-net supported membrane dams. Design drawing: Frei Otto, 1962

Page 170
Drawings and Photographs from IL 11 Light structures and energy technology.
Ill. 2,3: Model studies for the minimal surface cooling tower, IL, Frei Otto (see chapter on net constructions).

Page 171
Ill. 5:   Bic-l diagram, 1985 version. The most recent version is to be found in IL 14 Das Prinzip Leichtbau.
Ill. 6:   Project for a water tower. Model study: Frei Otto, 1962. Photograph: Frei Otto.
Ill. 7:   Suspended flexible containers for liquids and bulk materials. Model study: Frei Otto, 1962. Photograph: Frei Otto.

Page 172, 173
Moving cover for harmful waste dumps, design 1994: Frei Otto with Ingrid Otto, Christine Otto-Kanstinger, Bodo Rasch with B. Gawenat, S. Greiner. Engineers: E. happold, Bath. Photographs and drawings: Atelier Frei Otto, Warmbronn.

Page 174
Ill. 1:   Sunshade machine with model of the umbrellas (ill. 2) for a hexagonal lattice shell for the Kocommas project, which was planned but not executed. (See chapter on shells, p. 141).
Ill. 3,4: Shade in the desert, 1972. Architects: Atelier Frei Otto, Warmbronn, Frei Otto and Ewald Bubner with A. Bienhans, D. hadjidimos, A. v. Lieven, R. Gutbrod with h. Kendel. Engineers: Ove Arup and Partners, London, P. Rice.
Page 175
Ill. 6,7: Convertible umbrellas, 5m x 5m, for the roof of the haram Mosque in Makkah, Saudi Arabia. Architects: Bodo Rasch with J. Bradatsch,

R. holzapfel, 1987. Engineers: Mayr + Ludescher, Stuttgart. Client: Saudi Binladin Group, Jeddah. Two groups of prototypes have so far been built. (See chapter 0 umbrellas, pp. 188. 189). Photographs: SL Archive.

Page 176, 177
Studies for climate regulation with convertible roofs.
Ill. 1: 1 Study as part of a design for a toldo as a shade in the inner courtyard of the King Saud Mosque in Jeddah. Bodo Rasch with J. Bradatsch, 1988. Climate research: W. haaf (see p. 183). Drawings: SL Archive.
Ill. 2,3: Illustration to clarify climate regulation with a toldo in the inner courtyard of the Quba Mosque in Saudi Arabia. Design: Bodo Rasch with J. Bradatsch, 1988.   Toldo construction: J. Schilling. Climate research: W. haaf. Drawings and photographs: SL Archive.

Page 177
Study of climate regulation by convertible umbrellas in the inner courtyards of the Mosque of the Prophet in Madinah, Saudi Arabia. The shades, convertible umbrellas and Sliding Domes are described in more detail in the chapters on Makkah and Madinah (pp. 191-194, 206-213). Climate research: Architektur-büro Bodo Rasch, Ossama Bassiony, W. haaf. Drawings and photographs: SL Archive.

Literature: IL 11 Lightweight and Energy Technics, Frei Otto: Natürliche Konstruktionen, DVA Stuttgart, 1982.

Convertible Constructions

Page 179
Ill.:   Project study for a convertible roof over a multimedia stadium for Farbwerke hoechst. Design: Frei Otto with B. Burkhardt, M. Eckhout, R. Plate, Bodo Rasch 1971. Multiple exposure of the opening and closing process: Frei Otto.

Page 180
Ill. 1,2: Student project at IL, 8/1984. Photograph: IL Archive.
Page 181
Ill. 3:   Traditional toldos providing shade in the streets of Cordoba, Spain. Photograph: IL Archive, SL Archive.
Ill. 4:   Toldos in the inner courtyard of the

Uthman Katkhuda mosque, Cairo. Photograph: IL Archive.
Ill. 5:   Convertible structure over the casino of the Masque de Fer open-air theatre in Cannes. Architects: Frei Otto with B. F. Romberg, A. Edzard, R. Taillibert, 1965. Engineers: S. du Chateau, Paris. Execution: Queffelec, Paris, L. Stromeyer + Co. GmbH. Photograph: Atelier Frei Otto, Warmbronn.

Page 182
Ill. 1,2: Convertible roof for the open-air theatre in the Stiftskirche, Bad hersfeld. Architects: Frei Otto, E. Bubner, U. Röder, 1968. Engineers: Leonhardt + Andrä. Execution: Felten und Guilleaume, Carlswerk AG, Cologne, C. haushahn, Stuttgart, Steffens und Nölle GmbH, Berlin, L. Stromeyer + Co. GmbH, Konstanz. Photograph: IL Archive, Atelier Frei Otto, Warmbronn.

Page 183
Ill. 3-5: Convertible roof for the open-air theatre in Wiltz, Luxemburg. Architects: Bodo Rasch with J. Bradatsch, 1988. Execution: KOIT high-Tex, Rimsting. Photograph: SL Archive.

Page 184
Ill. 1:   Extension curve and model of the "Cabrio" folding stan cover. Architects: Bodo Rasch with A. Walz, B. Gawenat. Execution: Götz Gmbh, Stuttgart. Photograph: SL Archive.
Ill. 2:   Project study for a convertible roof for a multi-media stadium for Farbwerke hoechst. Design: Frei Otto with B. Burkhardt, M. Eckhout, R. Plate, Bodo, Rasch 1971. Multiple exposure of the opening and closing process: Frei Otto.

Page 185
Ill. 3:   Climate regulation study with convertible roof shades. Part of a toldo design for the King Saud Mosque in Jeddah. Architects: Bodo Rasch with J. Bradatsch, 1988. Climate testing: W. haaf. Drawings: SL Archive.
Ill. 4,5: Toldo for the inner courtyard of the Quba Mosque, Saudi Arabia. Design: Bodo Rasch with J. Bradatsch, 1987. Execution: J. Schilling.

Literature: IL 5 Convertible Roofs, IL 7 Shadow in the dessert, IL 29 The Tent City of the hajj, IL 30 sun and shade .

Umbrellas

Page 187
Ill.: Convertible umbrellas in the inner courtyard of the Mosque of the Prophet in Madinah, Saudi Arabia. Architects: Dr. Kamal Ismail, Bodo Rasch with J. Bradatsch, R. Kollmar, 1991. Engineers: happold Office, Bath. Client: Kingdom of Saudi Arabia, represented by the Saudi Binladin Group, Jeddah. Execution: SL GmbH. Photograph: SL Archive.

Page 188–189
Ill. 1: Japanese umbrella. Photograph: SL Archive.
Ill. 2,4,5: Convertible umbrellas at the Bundesgartenschau in Cologne, 1971. Architects and engineers: Frei Otto with Bodo Rasch, A. Linhart, h. Isler. Execution: Schenker, Stromeyer+Co., Konstanz. Photographs: Atelier Frei Otto, Warmbronn.
Ill. 3,6,7: Umbrellas for Pink Floyd. Architects and engineers: Atelier Frei Otto, Warmbronn, Frei Otto with N. Goldsmith, G. Wright, h. Doster, happold Office, Bath, 1978.

Page 190–191
Ill. 1–4: Convertible umbrellas, 5m x 5m for the roof of the haram Mosque in Makkah, Saudi Arabia. Architects: Bodo Rasch with J. Bradatsch, R. holzapfel, 1987. Engineers: Mayr + Ludescher, Stuttgart. Client: Saudi Binladin Group, Jeddah. Two prototype groups have been executed to date. Photographs: SL Archive.

Page 192
Ill. 1–3: Convertible umbrella, 10m x 10m. Architects: Bodo Rasch with J. Bradatsch, R. holzapfel, A. Walz, B. Gawenat, 1987. Engineers: happold Office, Bath. Client: Saudi Binladin Group, Jeddah. Execution: SL GmbH. Photographs: SL Archive.

Page 193–197
Ill.: Convertible umbrellas in the inner courtyard of the Mosque of the

Prophet in Madinah, Saudi Arabia. Architects: Dr. Kamal Ismail, Bodo Rasch with J. Bradatsch, R. Kollmar, 1991. Engineers: happold Office, Bath. Client: Kingdom of Saudi Arabia, represented by Saudi Binladin Group, Jeddah. Execution: SL GmbH . Photograph and drawings: SL Archive, Saudi Binladin Group.

Literature: IL 16 Tents; IL 5 Convertible roofs, exhibition catalogue "Schirme", Rheinlandverlag, 1992.

Makkah and Madinah
Work for the holy places

Page 199
Ill.: Night photograph of the Mosque of the Prophet in Madinah, Saudi Arabia. Photograph: Saudi Binladin Group, 1993.

Page 202
Ill. 1: Muna valley during the hajj. Photograph: SL Archive, from: IL 29 Zeltstädte, dissertation by Bodo Rasch, 1980.

Page 203
Ill. 2: Frei Otto's master-plan for Muna, competition entry, 1974. Architects: Frei Otto with S. Angawi, Bodo Rasch. Drawing from: IL 29 Zeltstädte, dissertation by Bodo Rasch, 1980.

Page 204
Ill. 1: View of a tented city during the hajj. Photograph: SL Archive, from: Zeltstädte, dissertation by Bodo Rasch, 1980.
Ill. 2,3,4: Prototypes of the frame tent on the mountain slopes near Muna. Architects: Frei Otto, Bodo Rasch, S. Angawi, 1981. Prototypes executed by: hajj Research Centre. Photographs: SL Archive.

Page 205
Ill. 5,6,7: Sanitary facilities for the tented cities. Design: Bodo Rasch with R. holzapfel, A. Walz, 1982, not executed.
Ill. 5: Fresh water container, pneumatic construction. Photographs: SL Archive. Literature: IL 29 Zeltstädte, dissertation by Bodo Rasch, 1980.

Page 206
Ill. 2,3: Pilgrims during the hajj. Photograph:

SL Archive, from: IL 29 Zeltstädte, dissertation by Bodo Rasch, 1980.

Page 207
Ill. 2,3,4: Computer simulation of the streams of pedestrians, Bodo Rasch with B. Gawenat, S. Al-Zoubi , Arscimed, Paris and Engineering Systems International, Paris.

Page 208, 209
Ill.: Convertible umbrellas in the inner courtyard of the Mosque of the Prophet in Madinah, Saudi Arabia. Architects: Dr. Kamal Ismail, Bodo Rasch with J. Bradatsch, R. Kollmar, 1991. Engineers: happold Office, Bath. Client: Kingdom of Saudi Arabia, represented by Saudi Binladin Group, Jeddah. Execution: SL GmbH. Photographs: SL Archive, Saudi Binladin Group, Jeddah.

Page 210–215
Ill: Sliding Domes over the inner courtyards of the Mosque of the Prophet in Madinah, Saudi Arabia. Architects: Dr. Kamal Ismail, Bodo Rasch ,R. Bühler, N. Stone, 1991. Engineers: Mayr + Ludescher, Stuttgart. Client: Kingdom of Saudi Arabia, represented by Saudi Binladin Group, Jeddah. Execution: SL GmbH, Saudi Binladin Group, Jeddah.

Page 216–221
Ill.: Lighting for the great piazza surrounding the Mosque of the Prophet in Madinah, Saudi Arabia. Architects and Engineers: Dr. Kamal Ismail, Bodo Rasch, J. Bradatsch, W. Kestel, B. Ditchburn. Lighting technology: C. Bartenbach, Innsbruck.Large convertible umbrellas (23m x 23m) in the piazza surrounding the Mosque of the Prophet in Madinah. Architects and engineers: Dr. Kamal Ismail, Bodo Rasch, J. Bradatsch, R. Kollmar, h. Voigt, S. Greiner, W. haase, F. Wondratschek.

Page 222,223
Time exposure to examine the movement of pilgrims during the ritual circling of the Kaaba in the courtyard of the Al haram Mosque in Makkah. Study: Bodo Rasch with B. Gawenat. Photograph: SL Archive.

Literature: Il 29 The Tent City of the hajj.